Upper Access, Inc.
Hinesburg, Vermont

Other books by Don Nedobeck:

Nedobeck's Alphabet Book
Nedobeck's Numbers Book
The 12 Days of Christmas
No Known English Translation

Upper Access Books
One Upper Access Road
P.O. Box 457
Hinesburg, Vermont 05461
802-482-2988
(Book ordering information) 1-800-356-9315

Library of Congress Cataloging-in-Publication Data

Edwards, Pat, 1951-
    Cheap eating : how to feed your family well and spend less / by Pat Edwards ; illustrated by Don Nedobeck.
        p.   cm.
    Includes index.
    ISBN 0-942679-10-5 (alk. paper : pbk.) : $9.95
    1. Marketing (Home economics) 2. Low budget cookery. I. Title.
    TX356.E38 1993   92-36221
    641.3' 1--dc20   CIP

Printed on acid-free paper.

For Bob, who believes in me and makes it so.

Acknowledgments

I thank my parents for showing me how to do it right. I'm especially grateful to my husband, Bob, for putting up with my experimentation, and to my two sons, William and David, who will eat anything, and have. I also thank Barb for her bread, Diana for her mayonnaise, Katie for her frequent trips to visit the squirrels (which gave me much-needed breaks), and Lisa for her insights on toilet paper. Each one brightened my day and lightened my task. Thanks also to those co-workers who allowed me to use them as guinea pigs and sounding boards.

Contents

Introduction

I'm baffled by the negative connotation often attributed to the word "cheap." Cheap means getting something for a lesser price, right? Webster says it's "inexpensive," or "costing little to obtain." Sounds like smart business to me!

Somehow, the word "cheap" has been confused with the word "inferior." This is a misconception, at least in the area of food. Spending more money does not make food tastier or more nutritious. Most American families could eat better than they do now, for far less money than they now spend.

To be honest, I started this book when I was broke and hungry. The financial struggle jolted me into rethinking food issues. Oh, I had things to eat, but I was fresh out of imagination, and there didn't seem to be anything that didn't remind me of how broke I was. A jelly sandwich may hit the spot now and then if that's what you feel like, but not if that's all you feel you can afford!

What I learned is just as useful in good financial times as in bad. Even if you can afford to waste money, why would you want to? If you save money on food, there's more left for other things. Even millionaires don't stay that way by being spendthrifts!

Cheap eating is certainly not a new idea. It's a talent that all human cultures seem to learn and relearn during hard economic times. For example, an earlier generation of Americans survived the Great Depression, thanks in part to cheap eating. Many continued their frugal ways after the economy improved—and prospered as a result. They could take better advantage of their new "wealth" because they didn't waste it.

Unfortunately, much of that wisdom has been forgotten or set aside by our generation. Many families are working extra jobs, and sacrificing other needs or wants, in order to support expensive eating habits.

Of course, times do change. Compared to times past, fewer of us now have the ability to raise a cow in the backyard. Most of us aren't able to spend as many hours in the kitchen as Grandma did, even if we wanted to. And some of the foods once regarded as staples, such as lard, have rightfully fallen into disfavor.

So we can't just resurrect all the old ideas.

1

It's also important to keep in mind that most families are probably not prepared for fundamental changes in their diets. A well-planned vegetarian diet (for example) can be both cheap and healthful. If you're willing to make that commitment, more power to you! But the focus of this book is not to convince you to change your tastes in food. The goal is to eat the way *you* want to eat, while saving money.

I've learned to enjoy being cheap. I enjoy saving money for a trip to New England, or a new bicycle, or a case of fine wine. Now, when people accuse me of being cheap, I say, "Thank you."

I hope that, by the time you finish this book, you'll agree. Cheap eating is smart eating. Together, perhaps we can restore "cheap" to its proper, dignified place.

Chapter 1
Ten Commandments for Cheap Eating

Cheap eating requires some self-discipline. Don't worry too much about the title of this chapter—I'm not passing along anything here that's engraved in stone for all time. But it's good to start with some basic money-saving ideas, and then follow them, well, religiously.

Perhaps, by the time you finish this book, you'll want to draw up your own list of "commandments," adapted to your own tastes and family. Then order yourself to abide by them. You'll be amazed at how much money a few self-imposed "Thou Shalt Nots" can save!

Below are ten of the simple commandments that I order myself to follow. If any seem appropriate to you right now, perhaps they can help you to make a fast start toward the lofty goal of cheap eating.

> **These "commandments" are self-imposed, so you'll want to make up your own.**

1. Avoid habit buying.

Don't let any of your commandments keep you from finding new bargains—look for alternatives that may be cheaper and better.

Some of my friends always shop at the same grocery store. They seem as loyal to "their" store as to their religion or political party. It is part of who they are. It gives their lives stability to know that on Friday night they will see the kids after work, fix a bite to eat, and go to their grocery. They've been shopping there since Susie and Sammi were little, and buying the same items. They've developed some highly ingrained habits.

> **If you shop on automatic pilot, you may be missing some bargains.**

Blind loyalty to brands can be expensive.

One of our dearest friends—a widower in his 70s—was a dedicated, dyed-in-the-wool, habit spender right up to his death a few years ago. Every week, his purchases at the store included Camay brand soap and facial tissues. At the time of his death he probably owned 48 bars of soap and as many boxes of tissues. Most of us don't go to such extremes in our habit buying, but our friend's example makes a point. Be sure you know why you're buying the things you are. "I always have" can get you in trouble—like buying powdered milk to save money and not noticing a price increase.

2. Don't buy expensive packages.

Beware of high-priced packaging.

Juice is cheaper in 46-oz. cans than in quart bottles, which are cheaper than the little boxes. (They're also a lot less mess. Little kids tend to squeeze the boxes, and the juice shoots out the straw.) Salt is cheaper in two-pound packages than in disposable shakers. Raisins are cheaper in the one-pound box than in the mini-boxes. Honey in a glass jar is cheaper than a cute plastic bear.

Okay, fancy packages may be convenient—they will save you a few seconds now and then. But keep in mind that you may be paying more for the packaging than for the contents.

Trash bills are rising drastically these days. But you can beat that if you pay only for containers that can be recycled. Most of the fancy packaging has mixed materials that can't be easily separated. So being cheap about which package you buy will be a good deed for the environment, too.

3. Never buy pre-sweetened anything.

If you're going to buy sugar anyway, why buy it at five times the price you would normally pay?

My favorite example is iced tea mix at $2.35 for 7½ quarts, compared to instant tea at $3.37 for 30 quarts. It costs 7¢ per glass to make iced tea with a mix and less than 3¢ per glass—including sugar—to make it with pure instant tea. (The sugar you add is less than a quarter of a cent per teaspoon.) Maybe saving 4¢ a glass doesn't seem like much to you, but here's what gets my goat. The iced tea mix contains 84¢ worth of tea. The other $1.50 is for 20 tablespoons of sugar (1¼ cups). Now, 1¼ cups of sugar weighs 10 ounces (I weighed it), and at $1.50 for 10 ounces I'd be paying $2.40 per pound for sugar or $12.00 for a five-pound bag! I don't like paying an outrageous price for anything!

If you watch the pennies, the dollars will take care of themselves.

4. Don't serve big hunks of meat with every meal.

Those of you who have households which include football players, longshoremen, lumberjacks, or just plain meat-and-potatoes folk—stop laughing! Even a life long habit of daily sirloins can be broken if the alternatives taste good.

Use less meat.

My formula:

- meat on Sunday and Wednesday
- casseroles on Monday and Thursday
  (using leftovers whenever available)
- pasta on Tuesday
- fish, eggs, or cheese on Friday
- soup and sandwiches on Saturday

The idea is that there is enough meat scattered throughout the week so that, when my family refuses to eat another noodle, we can brace up and remain cheerfully cheap.

The only bad meals are meals that are not planned. Vegetable soup can taste great if served with salad and garlic bread. A meat feast now and then can be worked into a frugal budget, but you have to spread it around.

5. Serve no main dish more than twice a month.
Let's face it. The worst part of sticking to a budget is being reminded of the fact at mealtime. But the problem is monotony—not the tight budget. Even steak gets old when you have it four times in two weeks.

There are thousands of foods and millions of ways to cook them. Why bore yourself with the same foods over and over? Any foods, including those that are extremely inexpensive, taste best if you have them only once in a while.

Use a variety of meals to avoid tedious menus.

6. Try house brands or generics.
For years, there were certain brands I would not buy because I didn't like the color of the labels. Or I didn't like the name of the brand or the sound of the word. Then I made a miraculous discovery: the things in the cans and boxes had absolutely no relationship to the look of the labels.

I started experimenting with house brands and generics. Some I liked, some I didn't, but I definitely started saving money. (Note: Store brands are not always cheaper. It's important to check weight and cost of all brands.) Always try the cheapest brand, and if it doesn't measure up, try the next cheapest, until you've found the lowest-cost product that is acceptable.

A generic brand product may be a name brand hiding in a plain wrapper.

The higher price of a "name" brand is *never* a guarantee of higher quality. The house brands and generics are often the same products, put out by the same companies, at much lower prices.

7. Use coupons wisely.

I am a firm believer in coupons. In a recent month, I gleaned from one issue of a Sunday paper (newsstand price $1) coupons totalling $2.15. Besides newspapers, other places to find money-saving coupons are magazines, product packaging, and handouts in grocery stores. You can even send away or telephone for them.

A coupon, however, is no good unless you normally buy the product anyway. If you have a coupon for instant coffee, but people in your family wouldn't drink the stuff if you paid them, then you might as well give the coupon to someone who does love instant coffee.

Coupons can be seductive to higher spending.

There are coupon clubs for the hard-core clippers. If you enjoy this, you might investigate joining one of these clubs. It takes some time, work, and space. But methodical, organized coupon clipping can lead to very substantial saving.

8. Avoid convenience foods.

This may not always be easy if you have three-month-old twins, a full-time job, and/or a broken leg. But *if* it's possible, avoid using convenience foods.

Look at the labels—they're largely chemicals that nobody can pronounce, understand, or digest. They are also, in almost every instance, *far* more expensive than foods you prepare yourself. If you're willing to spend an extra ten minutes in the kitchen, you can generally prepare a better tasting, more nutritious meal at less than half the price.

Pay yourself to do the cooking.

9. Purchase the largest packages you can store.

Check the unit pricing just to be sure, but in general, the larger the package, the cheaper the contents.

Bigger is usually better, but not always.

If you don't have a lot of storage room, you may have to be creative. Is there room under the bed? Canned goods will stack in cases, and, with a pretty table cover, who's to know it's not an end table? Meats and poultry can be divided into useable amounts and frozen or even canned.

But don't buy more than you'll use in a reasonable time period. In a fit of frugality, I once purchased a ten-pound bag of rice. That was only shortly before my mother-in-law, who had done the same thing, brought me a gift of four more pounds. It probably will keep forever (I feel as though it already has), but there's a doubt factor to deal with. We have even considered getting married again just to use up the last six pounds. My husband said he would rather find ways of eating it.

10. Always measure.

Okay, I know your mother just "dumps," and it turns out great. My mother does it, too, and taught me to do it. I have never ruined anything with my pinches and dabs. Except my budget.

Watch out for the "dumps."

When you don't measure, you have no reliable way of knowing whether you have added a teaspoon or a tablespoon, a cup or a quart. "Dumpers" almost always use more than they need, just to be sure that they have enough. If you use a half teaspoon of vanilla extract every time the recipe calls for a quarter teaspoon, you'll have to buy vanilla twice as often. Cumulatively, this practice will add to your food bill.

One of the worst perils of dumping is with laundry products. (Okay, I know, detergent isn't food. But if you buy it at the grocery store, the cost is melded into the food budget.) If you just dump, your clothes may get clean and white, but your money is going down the drain. It's amazing how much you can save just by measuring.

Chapter 2
Are You Disorganized?

In this life, there are doers and planners. The doers do, and the planners plan. Sometimes, the planners also do, and that's the best combination.

The doers plunge right in headlong with a zest for life and confidence that things can't be made much worse. How I envy them! I am a planner. I even have an alternative emergency plan for taking out the garbage.

As a planner, however, I have one advantage over the doers. When I saunter into the supermarket to spend my hard-earned cash, I am prepared. I have my list of exactly what I will be using this week, written on an envelope into which I have placed the money-saving coupons I will need for this week's purchases.

My list is exact and complete. It is laid out, not in alphabetical order, but in the order that I will encounter the items. That is, if my store has coffee and tea in the first aisle, I put them first on my list. This system can be modified according to the practical demands of transporting foods. For instance, frozen food should be purchased last to make sure it does not thaw. (Fortunately, most store managers understand that and have the decency to put frozen foods at the end of the maze.)

Actually, the place to start, when talking about food shopping, is not in the supermarket, but in the living room or study or wherever you prepare your menus. To eat cheap, you have to think cheap, and planning has always been a foundation for saving money. With 4,000 packages of

Do you plan your meals in the grocery aisles? If so, your budget is at risk.

9

Even a little planning is much better than no planning.

potato chips staring at you, it's easy to blow your budget if you aren't forearmed.

I admit that many people consider my planning to be extreme. Like the dieter who counts every calorie, I count every single cent. (I have a collection of pennies worth exactly 1¢ each. Their cumulative value is not yet significant, but they will buy dinner one day.)

If that level of planning seems like more than you can bear, don't give up. The steps listed here are suggestions, and if you follow them all, I'll guarantee big savings! But knowing that I'm an extremist on this issue, you may want to figure out a compromise that you can live with. Even a little planning is much better than no planning.

Menus

Eating has to be good for your family.

Once upon a time, I was working as a housemother at a private school for teenage boys. I was responsible for feeding 12 of the students twice daily, and when teenage boys are hungry, they are hungry all over. The meals had to be nutritionally sound as well as filling, and, at lunchtime, fast.

It took planning to get it right. But after charting the daily nutritional needs, it was simply a matter of dividing them over three meals a day. Then the only problem was getting the food served and on the table in time.

The latest recommendation (1992) from the Nutrition Information Service of the U.S. Department of Agriculture has increased the proportion of fruits, vegetables, and grain products we should be eating, which is good news for the thrifty shopper: This "Food Guide Pyramid"—in addition to promoting healthful eating—will make your shopping more affordable.

Food Guide Pyramid
A Guide to Daily Food Choices

ts, Oils, & Sweets
E SPARINGLY

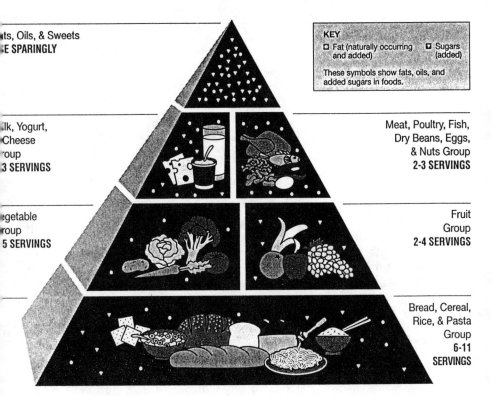

lk, Yogurt,
Cheese
'oup
3 SERVINGS

Meat, Poultry, Fish,
Dry Beans, Eggs,
& Nuts Group
2-3 SERVINGS

egetable
roup
5 SERVINGS

Fruit
Group
2-4 SERVINGS

Bread, Cereal,
Rice, & Pasta
Group
6-11
SERVINGS

The 6-11 servings of grain products are not as much as it sounds when you consider that one slice of bread equals one serving, but both halves of an English muffin or hamburger roll add up to two servings.

Bread, Cereal, Pasta, and Grain Group

(Eat 6-11 servings daily)

Food	Serving	Grams of fat
Bread, 1 slice	1	1
Hamburger roll, bagel, English muffin	2	2
Tortilla, 1	1	1
Rice, pasta, cooked, ½ cup	1	trace
Plain crackers, small, 3-4	1	3
Breakfast cereal, 1 oz.	1	check label
Pancakes, 4", 2	2	3
Croissant, 1 large, 2 oz.	2	12
Doughnut, 1 medium, 2 oz.	2	11
Danish, 1 medium, 2 oz.	2	13
Muffin, 1 medium, 2 oz.	2	varies
Cake, frosted, slice-16ths	1	13
Cookies, 2 medium	1	4
Pie, fruit, 2-crust, 6th	2	19

Someone in your family overweight? Try charting your menus, after the fact, to see what you've been serving.

Beware of kids' picky demands—they may want to skip "sparkle foods"—the high-vitamin vegetables everyone needs. With a little imagination, there are lots of ways to disguise veggies. Don't be intimidated into omitting them, or any other food group, either!

As long as you keep it simple, filling out a chart each day can be a quick and easy way to plan balanced meals until you have the hang of it.

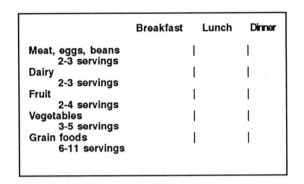

	Breakfast	Lunch	Dinner
Meat, eggs, beans 2-3 servings			
Dairy 2-3 servings			
Fruit 2-4 servings			
Vegetables 3-5 servings			
Grain foods 6-11 servings			

Shopping Lists

Once I have the menu for the week, it's time to start my shopping list. Taking a piece of lined paper, I list everything that I will need to prepare each meal. I leave out *nothing*! If a recipe calls for a flour coating, I write down flour. If it says "season to taste with salt and pepper," I write down salt and pepper. (Okay, I don't write down the salt and pepper for every single recipe, but I try to make a point of accounting for everything that will be needed for the week's menus.)

Detailed lists aren't for everyone, but try to be as methodical as possible.

Then I go to the kitchen and, pen in hand, go through cabinets, refrigerator, and freezer, crossing off everything I do not need. If I haven't used flour in a while, it's easy to forget that there are only three tablespoons left. Thoroughness at this point can help to avoid extra trips to the store, saving time and saving money on gasoline.

The unplanned purchases will ruin your budget!

After checking the snack shelf and non-food items like laundry detergent and toilet tissue, I add what I need, and my list is done. Time permitting, I may recopy it, because by now it's usually a mess.

Now, all I need is money and I'm ready to shop, right? Well, not quite. Let's take some time to determine the best place or places to shop.

Gas is part of Your Budget...
unless You ride a horse to the Stor[e]

Chapter 3
Where, When, and How to Shop

Where to Shop

With food, as with everything else, some places are better to shop than others. One store may have a well-kept produce section to seduce customers' loyalties. Another may always stock the best meats. All stores try to lure you with advertisements.

Advertising can be an effective way to attract shoppers to a store. I know lots of people who won't shop for groceries until the weekly ads come out in the newspapers.

But the ads mention only a few of the thousands of items that the markets carry. Once you get into a store, you'll probably spend a lot more on the items that aren't on sale. Sure, you can run from store to store buying sale merchandise, but are you spending a dollar on gas to save 35¢ on graham crackers? Do you know for sure that one grocery's sale price isn't another store's everyday price? Is this how you really want to spend your free time?

Gas is part of your food budget . . . unless you ride a horse to the store.

Thoroughly comparing prices at all your local markets can be time-consuming, but very worthwhile if you have time. The ideal is a methodical survey. And if you have a group of friends or neighbors to share the task, it can be fun.

The Ideal Way to Comparison Shop

First, make a list of items you buy regularly. A little later in this section, I'll suggest a basic list, but you'll want to modify it to account for

Shop without buying.

the items you buy regularly. Your list doesn't have to be exhaustive, just varied enough to be realistic.

Now comes the detective work. You and your friends will each pick a store to "shop." Cruise the aisles, noting the prices of every item on your list. If the manager asks what you are doing, you can cheerfully say, "I belong to the Smart Shoppers Club and I'm doing some comparison shopping for our membership." (I'd be inclined to give that answer even if I were the only member of the club.)

Ideally, you should track prices each week for a month to get a clear idea of the pricing pattern of each store. Does one store jack up its prices for a while just before a sale? What happens to prices around the first of the month, when a lot of people on fixed incomes do a monthly shopping for staples?

Once you crunch the numbers, you may find that the store you thought was cheapest is not.

One group found that while one store had better sales, the basic things such as flour and sugar were always more expensive. If you have time for only one shopping in a given week, you may choose the store you know will be cheaper for most of the things you need to buy. Or you may decide that it's worth stopping for the sales at one store and going on to the next for the rest of what you need.

Time-Saving Compromises

Even if you are working with a group of friends, you may not have the time to research prices as thoroughly as you'd like. In some communities, local consumer organizations do periodic price comparisons at area supermarkets and publish the results.

If not, and if you don't have time for thorough research, do your best to compare prices objectively. Try doing your weekly shopping at different stores, and take careful notes while you shop. After a few weeks, you'll have a pretty good idea of which stores offer the best prices on the items that you buy *regularly*.

But make an effort to be as methodical as possible. Your final bill at the cash register is no good for price comparisons, unless you really buy the same things each week. Take the time, while shopping, to check the prices of things that you sometimes buy, even though you are not buying them this week. Write those prices on a checklist, and later compare the prices of the various stores for each item.

The store that charges 3¢ less for milk may be the best place to shop, even if it charges 3¢ more for salt.

To determine the best places to shop, you'll have to adjust your findings to the quantities of items you normally purchase. If you have a growing family, milk probably consumes a much bigger part of your food budget than, say, table salt. So the store that charges 3¢ less for milk may be the best place to shop, even if it charges 3¢ more for salt. It's hard to weigh these issues with scientific precision, but do the best you can.

Suggested List for Comparison Shopping

Regardless of how you go about comparing prices, begin with a good, well-thought-out list of the things that you buy regularly. Scanning through the list on the next two pages may be helpful in preparing your own list. It's somewhat arbitrary but represents the items that a budget-conscious family with typical American tastes might choose. Feel free to copy it, if you'd like. (The chart will be easier to use if you enlarge it to about 140%.)

Comparison Shopping List

	Store 1	Store 2	Store 3
Sugar, white, house brand, 5 lbs.	_____	_____	_____
Sugar, dark brown, house brand, 1 lb.	_____	_____	_____
Sugar, house brand, 10 lb.	_____	_____	_____
Flour, white, house brand, 5 lbs., unit price	_____	_____	_____
Flour, white, house brand, 10 lbs., unit price	_____	_____	_____
Flour, white, house brand, 25 lbs., unit price	_____	_____	_____
Baking Soda, cheapest brand, 1 lb.	_____	_____	_____
Baking Powder, Rumford, 12 oz.	_____	_____	_____
Salt, house brand, 1 lb.	_____	_____	_____
Pepper, house brand, 8 oz.	_____	_____	_____
Cinnamon, house brand, 1 oz.	_____	_____	_____
Garlic powder, house brand, 1 oz.	_____	_____	_____
Garlic, fresh, per oz./lb.	_____	_____	_____
Vanilla extract, house brand, 2 oz.	_____	_____	_____
Mayonnaise, house brand, 32 oz.	_____	_____	_____
Mustard, house brand, 16 oz.	_____	_____	_____
Ketchup, house brand, 1 qt.	_____	_____	_____
Vegetable oil, house brand, 1 qt.	_____	_____	_____
Vinegar, house brand, 1 qt.	_____	_____	_____
Tomato paste, house brand, 6 oz.	_____	_____	_____
Tomato sauce, house brand, 1 qt.	_____	_____	_____
Spaghetti, house brand, 1 lb.	_____	_____	_____
Spaghetti, house brand, 3 lb.	_____	_____	_____
Elbow macaroni, house brand, 1 lb., unit price	_____	_____	_____
Elbow macaroni, house brand, 3 lb., unit price	_____	_____	_____
Rice, brown, River Brand, 1 lb.	_____	_____	_____
Beans, dried navy, house brand, 1 lb.	_____	_____	_____
Lentils, dried, house brand, 1 lb.	_____	_____	_____
Peas, dried split, house brand, 1 lb.	_____	_____	_____
Soup, tomato, house brand	_____	_____	_____
Soup, chicken noodle, dry, house brand	_____	_____	_____
Bouillon, beef, per box	_____	_____	_____
Bouillon, chicken, per box	_____	_____	_____
Saltines, house brand, per lb.	_____	_____	_____
Oatmeal, house brand, 1 lb.	_____	_____	_____
Puffed wheat, 1 lb.	_____	_____	_____
Bran flakes, 1 lb.	_____	_____	_____
Corn flakes, 1 lb.	_____	_____	_____
Peanut butter, chunky, house brand, 12 oz.	_____	_____	_____
Jelly, grape, house brand, 12 oz.	_____	_____	_____
Honey, house brand, 12 oz.	_____	_____	_____
Tomato juice, house brand, 48 oz.	_____	_____	_____
Apple Juice, 48 oz.	_____	_____	_____
Grapefruit Juice, 48 oz.	_____	_____	_____

	Store 1	Store 2	Store 3
Orange juice, frozen, house brand, 12 oz.			
Green peas, frozen, house brand, 10 oz.			
Green beans, frozen, house brand, 10 oz.			
Corn, frozen, house brand, 10 oz.			
Broccoli, frozen, house brand, 10 oz.			
Spinach, frozen, house brand, 10 oz.			
Potatoes, cheapest kind, 5 lbs., unit price			
Potatoes, cheapest kind, 10 lbs., unit price			
Potatoes, cheapest kind, 25 lbs., unit price			
Onions, cheapest kind, per lb.			
Bananas, per lb.			
Lettuce, iceberg, per head			
Green peppers, per lb.			
Celery, per bunch			
Cabbage, per lb.			
Carrots, per lb.			
Lemons, each			
Milk, 2%, house brand, 1/2 gallon			
Milk, 2% house brand, gallon			
Milk, powdered, house brand			
Half & Half, house brand, pint			
Butter, brick, house brand, per lb.			
Margarine sticks, house brand, per lb.			
Cheese, American, house brand, per lb.			
Cheese, cheddar, brick, house brand, per lb.			
Cheese, mozzarella, brick, house brand, per lb.			
Cheese, cream, house brand, 8 oz.			
Cheese, cream, house brand, 1 lb.			
Ground chuck, per lb.			
Chuck roast, per lb.			
Chicken, whole, per lb.			
Turkey, ground, per lb.			
Pork, ground, per lb.			
Pork roast, butt end, per lb.			
Bacon, cheapest kind, per lb.			
Bologna, house brand, per lb.			
Salami, house brand, per lb.			
Toilet paper, Scott brand, unit price/sheets			
Toilet paper, house brand, unit price/sheets			
Paper towels, house brand, unit price/sheets			
Paper towels, name brand, unit price/sheets			
Dishwashing liquid, Octagon, unit price per oz.			
Dishwashing liquid, house brand, unit price per oz.			
Laundry detergent, house brand, per lb./gal.			
Laundry detergent, cheapest brand, per lb./gal.			

Discount Markets

In our part of the country (Ohio) we are blessed with a discount supermarket chain, Aldi's. They sell only the 600 items most often used, with no name brands (unless they get a special deal). You bag your own purchases, and either bring your own bag or buy one. They accept only cash and food stamps—no checks or coupons. There are no prices marked on anything—just posted signs. There's no fresh meat—only packaged or frozen—and not much produce. But the prices are unbelievably low!

Even so, I still have friends who won't go there because they don't want to stand in line, or because it's not tidy enough, or because it means a second stop at another store for other items.

If you don't have a store like this in your neighborhood, someone is missing a business opportunity!

Perhaps the actual results of my shopping trip on August 22, 1992 will encourage you to look for such a store in your area. The bill was $26.46, as itemized on the next page. On the day of this buying frenzy, I splurged an additional $13.25 at another supermarket for some name-brand cereals, a can of coffee (for which I had $2 in coupons), and some fresh produce. I also spent $1.77 for ground beef at the local meat market. This brought the total to $41.48. Except for extra milk and bread, that was our budget for *two weeks*, for our family of four.

You will notice some items that are conspicuous by their absence. I didn't buy a lot of vegetables because I had bought a case-full a couple of weeks before. You'll also notice in the list some conspicuous deviations from principles discussed elsewhere in this book. I could have done without the paper towels. I could have made better cookies, and macaroni and cheese, from scratch. Homemade soup and pork and beans would have tasted better than the canned products on sale, at lower cost. And I certainly

20

Shopping at Aldi's, August, 1992	
1 pr. panty hose	.59
1 roll paper towels	.39
1 box tissues (for school)	.59
2 lb. noodles @ .49	.98
24 oz. vegetable oil	.79
2 lb. hot dogs @ .49	.98
2 lb. spaghetti	.79
2 lb. carrots	.59
4 boxes mac & cheese @. 29	1.16
1 lb. beef bologna	.99
1 lb. fish fillets (perch)	1.99
3+ lb. chicken, legs/thighs @ .39	1.23
46 oz. pineapple juice	.99
46 oz. vegetable juice	.79
2 cans tuna @ .49	.98
18 oz. peanut butter	1.29
10½ oz. bag marshmallow (mini)	.39
4 loaves bread @ .25	1.00
1 pkg. hot dog buns	.29
2 doz. eggs @ .58	1.16
1 box vanilla wafers	.89
2 lb. margarine @ .39	.78
1 box graham crackers	.79
1 gal. milk (3½%)	1.89
1 lb. salt	.19
½ gal. apple juice	1.29
3 cans pork & beans @ .29	.87
6 cans soup @ .29	1.74
Sub Total	$26.31
Tax	.15
TOTAL	$26.46

Sometimes it *is* cheaper to buy ready-made —but it's not as good or nutritious as your own recipes.

didn't have to invest in name-brand cereal to provide good breakfasts, even if the coupons offered a big saving.

Indeed, there *is* some danger in shopping at a store where the prices of everything seem cheap. With the hectic pace of modern family life, occasional indulgence in convenience is hard to pass up. There's nothing wrong with that.

But don't go overboard. Remember, if a prepared food product costs no more than what you would spend making the equivalent from scratch, it's not really equivalent!

A good example is the little boxes of "macaroni and cheese dinner." If you make your own macaroni and cheese, it would cost as much or more. But that's because you would use a lot more cheese. Look at the ingredients list—there's less "dehydrated cheddar cheese" than salt. Just a little more cheese than FD&C yellow no. 5 and 6 food coloring. If you used that little cheese, *your* macaroni and cheese would be a lot cheaper than the prepared product.

"Cheap" convenience foods are no substitute for home cooking.

Yet for a quick and easy side dish, the boxed product is cheap and convenient, and kids generally like it. Unless there are allergies in the family, the chemicals, in moderation, are probably not harmful. So abandoning the "do-it-better-yourself" philosophy now and then is certainly understandable! (Actually, I use two of the little cheese-mix pouches instead of one, add dry milk powder, and save the leftover macaroni from the second box for another meal.)

I've digressed a bit, but the point is an important one. Discount markets tend to be a cheap place to buy staples *and* some convenience foods. So when you shop there, stock up on the items you will use. But don't lose sight of the fact that "cheap" convenience foods are no substitute for home cooking.

Shopping Co-ops

Spices are almost always cheaper at a co-op.

One option to consider, for at least some of your purchases, is food co-ops. The basic idea is that members pool their resources to buy food in bulk, and then share the labor of stocking shelves, running the register, and all the other things that grocery stores do for you. Anyone willing to put in a few hours a week can join, and the savings can be substantial.

22

Most co-ops will also sell to nonmembers at a higher price, which is convenient for those who can't devote an hour or two each week. Even for nonmembers, prices may well be lower than those of the local food chain.

There are many different types of food co-ops. Some specialize in organic or unprocessed foods, or foods that are useful in a vegetarian diet. They may not be the cheapest source of food overall—for example, they may have organic whole wheat flour that costs more than ordinary white flour would cost at the supermarket. The major attraction of this type of co-op is that it allows you to be picky about your diet without paying exorbitant prices.

Don't confine your shopping to a super-market.

Other Places to Find Bargains

There are many opportunities to find bargains on specific items on your shopping list. For example, the "thrift shops" that serve as outlets for major bakeries offer day-old bread at prices that are half, or even less, of what you would pay for the same product at the supermarket. The bread is usually just fine—but the companies want to sell it fast before it becomes stale. If you have a freezer, you can save large amounts of money by buying day-old bread in quantity. Freezing seems to freshen it, especially if you eat it soon after thawing.

Roadside farm stands often have bargain prices on fresh produce, when it is in season. The prices vary a lot, partly because some roadside stands cater to people who want fresh produce and are willing to pay extra for it. But if broccoli, for example, is in season and very abundant, the motivation is to sell as much of it as possible, as fast as possible. That's the time to stock up on broccoli, particularly if you have a freezer. If you have a root cellar (or another cool dark place for

If you have to drive 25 miles to get a bargain on farm-fresh broccoli that only one person will eat, it's not a bargain any more.

23

storage), it's worthwhile to stock up on potatoes, carrots, and onions when they are in season.

There are ample yearly opportunities to pick your own apples, strawberries, and other fruits when they are in season. It can be a pleasant outing, and the prices are low. If you make apple sauce or strawberry preserves, do it when the main ingredients are in season!

With a freezer, you can take advantage of the savings on seasonal and bulk purchases.

Local slaughterhouses usually offer good prices on meat, if bought in quantity. If you don't have a freezer, you may not be able to store a side of beef. But perhaps you could pool the purchase with three or four friends and neighbors. You'll each get a sizeable amount of good meat at a very reasonable price.

Some of these options are discussed in more detail elsewhere in this book. But the point here is that smart shopping often extends beyond the supermarket. If you can stock up on specific foods at other locations, you can reduce the amount you spend weekly at the supermarket.

When to Shop

If your local super-market is open 24 hours a day, night-time shopping is one way to escape from the kids.

To beat the crowds and avoid having to take produce that everybody else in town has rejected, the best time of day to shop is in the morning. The best day of the week is any day but Friday, Saturday, Sunday, or Monday. If you work at a regular, 40-hour-per-week job, weekends may be the most convenient time to shop. But if there is any flexibility in your schedule, avoid weekends.

How to Shop

Before going to the store, it may be helpful to keep a few ground rules in mind.

1. Shop alone if possible. Children tend to whine and nag until you buy them what they saw advertised on TV.

24

2. Eat before you go, even if it's just a snack. Impulse-buying is hard to resist when you're hungry.

3. Never pick up anything you don't intend to buy. Studies have shown that you're more likely to buy if you touch, so don't touch.

4. *Always* use a list, prepared from a weekly menu and grocery store ads. Buy nothing that isn't on the list. (There are exceptions to this rule, such as if you need to make a substitution or there's a bargain that you know you will use. Usually, however, you will know about these by reading the newspaper ads.)

5. Check unit pricing (the orange label on the shelf) before deciding which of several to buy. Catsup that used to come in quart bottles now comes in 28-ounce containers that look *almost* as big. Make sure all labels are given in the same measurements: ounces and ounces, not ounces and quarts.

Some companies cheat with shrinking packages.

6. Carry a pocket calculator and add each item you pick up. This will let you know the cost before you reach check-out lines. It's embarrassing to have to put something back once it's been bagged. Set a spending limit and stick to it.

Honor your spending limit.

Understanding Labels

Companies label packages to give you information about the product inside and the company that makes it. Some information is required by law. Some is not. Some labels are true works of art. But keep in mind that great art is usually expensive to print, and the cost is passed on to consumers. Unless you're planning to pin the label to your wall, good food doesn't require an attractive label.

You can tell a great deal from a label. Laws require that the label include the name and address of the manufacturer or distributor. There may also be a telephone number to call for questions or problems. Weight or volume will be on the label. Ingredients also must be printed on the label in descending order, according to the percentage of content. This means that if the first ingredient listed is water, then water is the single largest ingredient by weight. If the first ingredient is sugar, then sugar outweighs any other single ingredient. This is important to remember when you comparison shop.

Foods with sugar added are almost always empty calories.

The price might be on the label. There may also be a spot to get your attention if the price has been reduced. The UPC symbol (Universal Product Code) or Bar Code is not the price set by the manufacturer, as many people think. It is simply a symbol that a computerized scanner can read, to tell the register to look in its memory for the price the store has entered for the product. (Incidentally, the store doesn't have to charge what the manufacturer suggests. For sales, it can be less. It can also be more.)

Nutritional details may be on the label, or there may be an address you can write to request the information. Manufacturers are obliged by law to provide this. Make comparisons among similar products. Often, a slightly higher price can mean markedly better nutrition. (Do not be fooled by products that cost an arm and a leg for "100% nutrition." All that means is that they've ground up a vitamin pill and jacked up the price. Remember, good nutrition is not, by definition, more expensive.)

Reading labels is a good way to find out about all the chemicals we're secretly being "forced" to eat.

Expiration Dates

Expiration dates may be included. "Best Use By" dates don't necessarily mean you'll die if you eat it one week later. The expiration date does mean that you should try to use the product soon, because otherwise the quality may begin to deteriorate. For highly perishable items, such as dairy products, the date tends to be more significant than for, say, cereals.

If the date is in the distant future, the product may contain large quantities of preservatives. I'm always suspicious of anything that says, "Best when eaten by June, 2008."

An expiration date in the distant future probably signifies a powerful chemical preservative.

Despite the limitations, it's a good idea to check the dates. One young man I knew found a package of hot dogs that had a date from a year earlier. When he pointed this out to the store manager, the manager offered to sell it at half price. The young man was prudent enough not to take him up on the offer. The shop soon went out of business.

On cans, there may be a series of numbers on either end. If a number doesn't look like a date, then it's probably an identification number for the batch or lot. Many products have a shelf life of two to four years. Expired date or not, if a can is rusted, bulging, or leaking air or product, throw it away. One woman I know opened an old (obviously very old) can of stewed tomatoes. They had spoiled and the contents of the can covered her in a smelly red spray at the first crank of the can opener.

Close-out bargain centers often offer good food for cheap, but be on the lookout for food that may be spoiled.

Her case was a bit extreme, but it gives you an idea of what can happen. The fact is that *any* time a can sprays out air or produce, *no matter how good it may look*, you should throw it out. It may be contaminated by botulism, a form of bacteria that can kill you.

Warnings and Cautions

This leads us to warnings and cautions that appear on the labels of some products. Pay attention to them. But if the product is a poison, don't put too much faith in the antidotes listed on the label. Call a poison control center, package in hand. If the poison control center serving your area is not nearby, there may be a toll-free number. Keep the number posted near the phone.

The poison control center is more trust-worthy than the label!

If you suspect food poisoning, grab the package, what's left of the food, and the victim —then get them to the hospital fast!

Savings

Special offers and coupons sometimes appear on a label. These may be "instant" savings that you remove and use at the cash register, or you may have to cut them off to save money on this or another product. Always check the inside of a label before throwing away the package or can. Special offers allow you to send away for everything from toys to cookbooks to cash.

Digressing just a bit, after you remove the label from an empty can, cut off both ends of the can and step on it, saving it for recycling. This will save money in your bill for trash disposal, and if enough people do it often enough, will help to save our environment as well. Some people make a point of never buying items in a container that can't be recycled.

Your trash bill is legitimately part of your grocery bill.

Warranties

Warranties may guarantee freshness or satisfaction. You usually need the sales slip or cash register receipt, so you might want to hold on to yours for a couple of weeks until you're sure you're satisfied. Most stores will exchange anything that isn't of good quality if you're polite.

Read Labels Carefully

Many of the benefits of label-reading are obvious, but others may require some practice in order to decipher important information quickly.

Here's an example. If the label on a box of crackers describes the product as "cheez crackers," you can bet that the crackers do not contain real cheese. They may have a cheese-like flavoring. But the spelling change is not just an effort to be cute. By law, manufacturers can't use "cheese" in a product description unless the product contains real cheese. So they use similar-looking words, in hopes that consumers won't notice the difference.

Cute spelling is probably hiding something terrible: a customer con job.

Another example is vanilla. Vanilla is vanilla, right? Wrong. Knowing the terminology on the labels can help you to make a quick determination of what you are buying. Vanilla is a bean. So if you are buying a bottle of liquid instead of a bean, the word "vanilla" must be qualified on the label. The label may say "pure vanilla extract" or "vanilla flavoring" or "imitation vanilla flavor." These are not different names for the same product.

Vanilla extract is the real stuff. It's expensive, but it's the strongest and most flavorful of the three. Vanilla flavoring means that the manufacturers have used vanilla extract to make this flavoring, but it isn't true vanilla. Imitation vanilla flavor means the manufacturer has whipped up the whole thing as a copy. There is no true vanilla anywhere in it—just chemicals.

Too many labels are the product of creative writing!

Imitation vanilla flavor is by far the cheapest. It comes in a large bottle, frequently around a pint, but it's cheaper than the little bottle of pure vanilla extract. That's because you have to use more to get any flavor. And the taste, while similar, won't be identical to real vanilla. Most people prefer the real thing.

30

Another example is chocolate milk mix. Chocolate comes in "pure instant cocoa," "chocolate drink mix," and "chocolate-flavored drink mix." One woman I know once bought a product with the word "Dutch" on the label. "Dutch" is often used as a descriptive word for good chocolate. The box had pictures of smiling children drinking brown liquid. When she made a glassful, it tasted pretty terrible. Only later, when she looked at the label, did she notice that the words "cocoa" or "chocolate" or even "chocolate-flavored" never appeared.

"Dutch" doesn't mean chocolate, and "flavoring" doesn't mean vanilla.

Let the buyer beware. If the label doesn't say it's chocolate, it isn't chocolate. The same goes for chocolate candy, as opposed to "chocolate-flavored" candy. There's a big difference in flavor as well as price. Chocolate-flavored chips also won't melt as well or taste as good as real chocolate chips in cookies.

Watch for the qualifiers. Often, the more wordy a manufacturer gets, the less there is of what you want to buy. Anything with "flavor" contains very little of the product. It's what you do when you make soup with a ham bone—you use only enough for flavor. That's fine, but if you sold your soup, you'd probably be honest enough not to try to convince your customers that there's a lot of ham in it.

Sometimes, you can't be sure what you're buying without taking the time to read the fine print.

Continuing with the same analogy, if you didn't even use a ham bone in your soup, you could claim that it has "artificial ham flavor." That would mean that you've left out the ham bone and added chemical imagination instead.

Canned juices and punches can also cause confusion. On the store shelves, you'll find "juice," "punch," "fruit juice drink," and "fruit drink." What's the difference?

Obviously, juice is just juice—100 percent. Fruit juice "drink" refers to a beverage using

"10% juice" isn't worth four times the price.

If your kids are going to drink something nutritionally worthless, try homemade root beer.

fruit juice as an additive but not necessarily a base. Usually, the fruit juice is added to sugar water and artificial flavor and color in a large enough quantity—maybe 10 percent or so—to add a little flavor and credence to the label. Don't get excited about buying drinks for the kids because they have 10 percent real fruit juice. Ten percent of a quart, or 32 ounces, is 3.2 ounces.

I don't think seven tablespoons of juice in 29.8 ounces of sugar water is enticing enough to spend extra money for. And yet every day, hassled, hurried parents shell out extra money without realizing that they've been conned. Not for lack of information—it's all there on the label, if you just take the time to look. If you don't, it can be an expensive way to buy water.

"Fruit drink" is a little more honest. It's a drink that's supposed to remind you of fruit. That's about it. It's mostly just chemicals and sugar—essentially, soda pop without the bubbles. Before I'd buy canned drink, I think I'd get some packages of powdered drink mix for 20¢ or 25¢ each, and mix in my own sugar and water. It's not nutritious, but if you intend to have the empty calories anyway, at least it's cheaper.

"Punch" can get a little tricky. You can be talking about a blend of juices, fruit drinks, or any combination. My only advice is to read the label for ingredients. But then, that's my advice for everything you buy.

Chapter 4
Cutting Corners the Smart Way

About Meat

Shopping for meat at the local grocery is an excellent way to spend a great deal of money very quickly, with very little to show for your trouble or investment. Meat can be very expensive. It is not something to buy recklessly.

In thinking about meat, the first thing you need to consider is the number of persons you are feeding. The next thing to think about is how far you expect the meat budget to go. I will buy sirloin for an intimate dinner for two, but I'll give it a little more thought if we're having 20 or 30 of our closest friends over. For them, a bowl of chili can be welcome on a winter night—chili from $5 worth of "on sale" hamburger from last September. If you can find a good deal, plan to freeze meat for later.

When buying meat (any kind), ground is the cheapest form. That's because it doesn't have to look as good as steak or roast does. A butcher can include tough cuts that would be unappetizing if they weren't ground up. The butcher can also add other things, such as extra fat, or soybeans. This is sometimes called T.V.P., or textured vegetable protein. It's really very good and worth trying. The vegetable protein is easier to digest and low in saturated fat. (If your store does not offer this combination, it's not hard to make it yourself.)

Next up the price ladder of red meats are also tough cuts—the underside and front quarters of the animal. These are the sections that do the

Compare the dollars per meal, rather than the price per pound.

Tough cuts
can be just
as good but
take longer
to cook.

hard work. They have little marbling and a lot of muscle. Such cuts require long, slow cooking, with added liquid to get them to turn out moist and tender. Examples are flank, brisket, and shank.

The most expensive cuts are steaks, chops, ribs, and roasts. They come from the neighborhood of the center back. They require less cooking, with little or no liquid. Near the bone, the meat has most flavor and marbling.

Red meat should not be eaten too often. The better cuts that have fat marbling, and the ground meats with added fat, are both high in cholesterol. Many of us enjoy a good steak now and then, but eating one every night is hazardous to both your health and your pocketbook.

Of course, you could always go the hot dog or cold cut route, but deli meats aren't cheaper and may be less healthful (most contain nitrites and salt). If you don't have a cookout planned or lunches to pack, it's best to avoid these meats.

But used with moderation and common sense, you can make good, low-cost meals from either red or deli meats. Consider chipped beef, for example. I buy it in jars (5 ounces for $2.39), not at the meat counter. It's not cheap—at this writing it's about $7.65 a pound at the deli. It also contains a lot of salt. But it stretches wonderfully. I serve creamed chipped beef on toast or biscuits. It tastes great and uses very little beef per person. Other spiced meats that stretch well are bacon, sausage, kielbasa, and ham.

If you don't
know how to
make perfect
gravy, I'll
teach you
how.

Sometimes it's thrifty to buy a large portion of meat such as a roast because you'll be getting several meals from it. The Sunday roast doesn't turn out to be an expensive purchase by the time you've had beef pot pie and a hearty soup, too.

It amazes me that some people say they don't know how to make gravy—it's *soooo* easy—

whether it's pot roast, pork, or chicken. Just make sure you've added a lot of water to the roasting pan while the meat is cooking. After removing the roast and extra grease floating on top, place the pan on a stove-top burner at medium heat. Fill a clean jar part way with water—about a cupful—and add two heaping tablespoons of flour. Cap it and shake the dickens out of it, till all the lumps are gone. Pour the flour mixture slowly into the simmering broth and stir constantly. (If you have a lot of liquid, you may need to add more flour.) Salt and pepper to taste.

In general, the best way to save money on meat is to combine it with other foods. Use the meat for flavor—plan the protein from vegetable or dairy sources. Casseroles, hash, spaghetti with meat sauce, and other dishes can be made with relatively small amounts of meat, yet taste good and meet the nutritional needs of your family.

Use meat mostly for flavor—plan additional protein from other sources.

In short, there are good alternatives to a regular, daily diet of steaks and roasts. Poultry and fish are among them, as are vegetarian meals. But if your family demands a regular dose of red meat, try to emphasize the casserole-type meals that use it in small quantities. Your budget, and your family's health, will be well served.

Non-meat sources of protein:

dried beans	dried peas
lentils	oatmeal
soy flour	cottage cheese
milk	eggs

About Poultry

It's hard to get stuck in buying poultry unless you buy an unclean or spoiling product. Smell the package. As far as price goes, the major differences come in convenience. When you buy separate chicken parts, you're paying for someone to cut up the bird. I save by buying a whole fryer and cutting it up myself. (But always check the cost per pound. If wings or thighs are cheaper than a whole fryer, I won't hesitate to buy them instead.)

Sometimes a store will lower the per-pound cost of a cut-up fryer by adding extra pieces. It *may* be a good deal, but I always check what's added. Almost always it's wings, necks, and extra giblets. If I buy them, I freeze the gizzards and hearts in one container, the wings separately, and the necks in a third container. After I have saved enough, I can prepare a meal of gizzards, another of chicken wings, and a pot of soup from the necks.

A "bargain" chicken may have three wings and two necks.

Most people cut a chicken into eight pieces — two wings, two thighs, two legs, and a split breast. It took me years to work up the courage to try cutting up a whole frying chicken. However, the idea of paying 10¢ or 15¢ cents more per pound for a cut-up fryer finally goaded me into trying.

But emotions do argue with intellect when you decide how "cheap" you're willing to be. For example, I always buy "dressed" whole fryers. If you're planning to buy an "undressed" whole chicken from the farmer, you'll have to clean it yourself, which means removing the internal organs. I'm not up to that point yet!

The ingredients required for cutting up a whole fryer are: (1) a whole fryer, (2) a *very* sharp knife, and (3) patience. I start with the legs. Holding a leg by the bottom (foot end), twist it up and toward the back to disjoin it from the thigh. When you have separated the joint, insert the point of your knife between the leg and thighbones to locate the separation, then cut the leg away from the thigh with one straight cut. Repeat with the other leg. Now disjoint the thighs in the same way as the legs, and cut between the separations to remove.

The wings should be removed at the body of the chicken (not at the first joint of the wing) by disjointing and cutting through the separations, as with the legs and thighs.

At this point you have the choice of cutting your fryer into eight pieces or, as some of the fried chicken restaurants do, into nine pieces. If you choose nine pieces, you'll have two rib portions (which extend from where the ribs join the breast bone around to the split back) and the boneless "keel" or center breast. Cut through the rib section, where the ribs join the breast bone, straight back toward the center of the back bone, and separate.

If you decide to have eight pieces, simply cut directly through the breast bone (which is mostly gristle, not bone), then cut through the ribs and remove the backbone.

The first time I ever roasted a turkey, my husband's grandmother was visiting and teaching me the fine points of turkey cooking. My first bird was ceremoniously christened "Tommer Etta Etacorn," and we set about cleaning and stuffing this magnificent Thanksgiving creature. To the confusion of grandmother, however, no giblets could be found. We checked thoroughly and finally decided that someone else's dinner would be resplendent with Tommer Etta's giblets.

The fragrance of roasting turkey that year was somewhat unusual. We couldn't quite place it, but it was vaguely reminiscent of hot paper.

Old-fashioned "black" knives are much easier to sharpen than stainless steel ones. Look for them at bargain prices at a garage sale—then learn how to use a sharpening stone.

37

If your family begins to get tired of turkey meals, try nickel-bone soup. Pay the kids 5¢ for each bone they find—it's still a cheap meal!

Dinner time came and a fine-looking turkey we had! My husband's carving, however, was somewhat hampered by a small paper pouch of well-roasted giblets tucked neatly into the neck cavity. To this day, I always check both the body and the neck cavity—with a chuckle.

Some people throw out the giblets. But together with the back, they can be made into a lovely pot of chicken or turkey noodle soup which costs almost nothing. That, my friends, is eating cheap!

About Fish

Buying fish is very much like buying other meat. If it's ground or formed or breaded so you can't see what it looked like before, it may cost less per pound, but there's less actual fish fillet per pound. A lot of those convenience foods are weighted down with bread crumbs and filler. What you're paying is not a cheap price for bread crumbs and filler.

If fish has been frozen, it won't float in water—one way to test if the fish isn't fresh.

If you buy fresh fish, ask the nice person at the fish counter for the best buy. He or she will be glad to talk to someone who isn't swimming. Fresh fish should be clear of eye and (usually) very white of flesh with a mild odor. The flesh should be firm to the touch (remember that fish can break down very quickly), and the scales should be shiny and firmly attached to the body.

Sometimes stores will try to sell fish that has been frozen and thawed. If you buy this (and there's no reason not to) be sure to cook it immediately. *Never* refreeze thawed fish. How can you tell if it's been frozen? Ask. If the clerk doesn't know, or if you don't absolutely trust the person, you can test the fish by putting it in water. Fresh fish will float.

38

> If you're worried about fish being tainted by mercury or pesticides, use the fillets only. Avoid fatty tissue. Smaller, young fish have had less time to absorb contaminants.

You can always catch your own, although this is not everybody's idea of a good time. Even if you don't fish, there may come a time when somebody you know hands you some of the extra catch-of-the-day. In my experience, people who offer you fish do not take "no" for an answer. If you're committed to cheap eating, and if you like fish, you'll thank your friend for the gift and make good use of it.

Those in your family who like to catch fish should learn how to clean them.

Depending on the type of fish, you may have to scale it. Thoughtful fishermen will gut the fish before passing on the catch to the kitchen, but don't count on it. One of the reasons people give fish away is that they enjoy catching them but not cleaning them. Don't feel bad if all this puts you off. If you can't stand the idea of cleaning freshly caught fish, or don't have the time, you can secretly bury them in the garden. Fish make great fertilizer.

About Fruits and Vegetables

Shopping for vegetables and fruits at the local supermarket is *not* the same as shopping at the farmers' market or at a roadside stand. At the grocery store, the produce is often done up in those little cardboard or polystyrene trays, which have a sneaky way of hiding the bad side of the produce. Even the see-through trays can fool you if bad spots are bundled up with nice fruits or vegetables in the same package.

Do you know how to find the cheap green pepper?

One way to get something for nothing is to find the heaviest.

Root crops are the cheapest.

One problem with grocery produce is that it's usually several days old. Produce starts losing its nutritive value quickly. If it's picked at 6 a.m. and in canning jars or the freezer by three p.m. the same day, that's fresh. But this doesn't often happen. Shopping separately for produce that is in season (for example, at a farm market) takes time. But it gives you the advantage of freshness and usually the saving of buying in bulk.

There's quite a range of weight in green peppers of the same size—*but* it's all in the innards which most people discard. So if you're paying per-pound, the lightest pepper may be the best deal. Sometimes you can just balance a pepper in each hand without running to the scale to find the better bet. But if the price is per-item (per head of lettuce, bunch of celery, melon, etc.) rather than per-pound, you want the heaviest.

When buying prepackaged vegetables or fruit (such as apples, carrots, onions, and potatoes), weigh those, too. If a bag of potatoes is ten pounds for $1.59, do you think a bit of potato has been shaved off to make it hit the mark exactly? Of course not, so find the bag that's going to give you the most extra for your money. (This hint came from *The Banker's Secret Newsletter*. See appendix.)

Of all plant food, root crops are the cheapest. Perhaps this is because they "do their own thing," with less work than some of the more exotic vegetables, usually with a plentiful harvest. Potatoes, onions, carrots, parsnips, turnips, and beets—are good "keepers." But don't store potatoes and onions together—the potatoes will spoil faster.

Potatoes provide a source of vitamin C as well as starch. There are endless uses in the American diet for potatoes, from breakfast food to dessert. Did you know that potatoes can be used for pet food, too? According to a recipe in *Bone Appétit* (New Chapter Press), Irish sheep dogs thrive on such goodies as mashed potato balls.

Kids are a good reason to own more than one peeler.

If you need a reminder about the instant kind: each serving of mashed potatoes probably costs 10¢ or more. With a good buy, in season, fresh potatoes will be half of that—and no chemicals. Too busy to think about peeling potatoes? Buy an extra peeler and let the others pitch in—it makes for quality time together.

Beets and turnips have the added advantage of greens—their leafy tops can be cooked and eaten. As with spinach, greens are very high in iron and vitamins. Some folks throw away the tops. What a waste! From a couple of bunches of beets, I can prepare boiled beets, greens, red beet jelly, and pickled beets with eggs. Shredded fresh beets are a lovely addition to a tossed salad or used instead of lettuce in a sandwich. One friend I know makes beet wine—it has a beautiful color and doesn't taste like beets at all—and the cooked beets are "leftover!"

Beets and cabbage are versatile foods that deserve more respect.

Cabbage is another underrated vegetable. From one large head—a dollar or two—I make stuffed cabbage, coleslaw, and a large kettle of ham and potatoes with cabbage, with scraps left over for a stir-fry. And cabbage can be canned or frozen.

Tomatoes are one of my all-time favorite bargains, as long as I can buy them in bulk, when they are in season. Real garden tomatoes taste much better than greenhouse tomatoes. Beware of "gas-ripened" tomatoes, which have been treated with a gas to turn them red a few days before they are really ripe. I wait for local tomatoes for my salads. For making paste, Italian "plum" tomatoes have less juice and fewer seeds.

Apples and bananas, in most parts of the country, are the best fruit bargains, unless you

41

are near a pick-it-yourself farm in fruit season. Or check with the produce manager for "spoiled" fruit (except citrus). You might even get some for free. A pear with a large, dark mushy spot may still have lots of firm flesh on it, and well-ripened fruit makes the sweetest fruit salad or compote.

Cheap canned vegetables may be false bargains.

Because of the extreme heat needed in the canning process, canned fruits and vegetables have less vitamin value than when frozen. You can see the difference especially in green vegetables. The three-for-a-dollar cans of green beans are not necessarily a bargain.

About Bread

There are probably more chances to save money in buying breads and cereals than in any other area.

The cheapest bread in the store isn't always the best buy.

Beware of false bargains. Store-variety white bread is cheaper than firm, brown bread. That's largely because it's 90 percent air! Try taking a piece of fresh white bread and compress it into a ball in your hand. That's what happens to it in your digestive system. It's about as healthful as play-dough or wallpaper paste. Health versus price is a consideration here. You'll do a lot better with a firm loaf that won't get crushed at the bottom of your shopping bag.

The cheapest, most healthful bread is home-made. I make my own bread, and the cost is a fraction of what I would have paid for anything better than the cheap white bread at the grocery store. Best of all, I know exactly what's going into it—which means no sodium benzoate or other weird ingredients. The aroma and flavor of home-baked bread can add quality to the dowdiest of meals.

Short of baking your own bread, the best way to save money is to buy day-old bread—in bulk—

on days when there are good deals at the bakery thrift shop. The bread isn't really stale when you buy it—the bakery is just unloading its surplus before it becomes stale. If you freeze it, then eat it shortly after thawing, it will taste even fresher.

What about mixes? An average muffin mix in my area goes for about $1.79. These mixes usually include flour, sugar, some type of leavening, seasoning, and a whole lot of chemicals. This doesn't include your own egg and sometimes oil! By contrast, it costs only about 50¢ to make a batch of muffins from scratch. When you're in a hurry, it's tempting to use a mix. But why not prepare your own mixes ahead of time? Check the recipe section.

Homemade muffins are the penny-pincher's best-kept secret!

Incidentally, one of the advantages of using muffins at a meal instead of bread is that you can add a lot of nutritionally healthful variety to the mix, including fiber.

Buying frozen waffles might be limited to only those times when the kids are serving you breakfast in bed. Since store waffles can be heated in the toaster, they are fairly safe and easy for kids to prepare. But you can obtain the same advantages by making waffles in advance and putting them in the freezer. Make up a large quantity, and the kids can pop them in the toaster whenever they want. Whole-wheat waffles are especially nutritious.

Freeze your own waffles.

Trick for rehabilitating "stale" muffins and breads: Put them into a brown paper bag, fold it closed, and drench the outside with cold water. Place in the oven (about 350°) for ten minutes or so. If using a microwave, avoid running it more than 30 seconds or so—to avoid toughness *or* a fire.

Cereals

I never buy pre-sweetened cereals (or pre-sweetened anything else for that matter). The cost per pound of sugar added to breakfast cereal is truly exorbitant. Sometimes, the price comparisons are confusing—the sweetened cereals cost a little less per pound. That is because much of the weight consists of sugar. If the unit price is $3 or $4 per pound, that's a lot to spend for sugar! Why not just add your own, at a fraction of the cost?

Why would anyone pay $4 a pound for sugar?

In fact, even unsweetened cereals can be extremely pricey, if you go beyond the basics such as house-brand corn flakes. The grains they are made from are cheap, but the processing and packaging multiply that price to well over $2 per pound—often over $4.

It's worth checking out some of the inexpensive cereals that you might not have tried for a while. For example, puffed wheat or puffed rice. The cheap brands often come in silly plastic bags that spill all over the shelf once opened. But it's not hard to overcome that problem. I use a one-gallon (restaurant size) jar. You can often get the jars free at the delicatessen.

Adding your own cinnamon and raisins to cooked rice, cracked wheat, or almost any grain (often cheapest at a co-op) makes good hot cereal at a fraction of the cost of box cereal.

How many bowls of cereal do you think you're getting from just one box?

If you want an interesting surprise, figure out how many bowls of cereal you actually get from one box. Sure, the nutritional information on the box describes dainty little one-ounce "servings." But for a teenager, a typical serving is likely to be four ounces or more—about four bowls of cereal from a 16-ounce box! That puts the cost at more than 50¢ a bowl *before* adding milk and honey. You can feed muffins to the whole family at that price.

44

Cold cereal is the creation of crafty market-eers who have convinced a generation of TV watchers that it's an American staple. Our great-grandparents didn't eat cold cereal for breakfast, and few people do in other countries.

Breakfast without cold cereal is not un-American!

Compare the per-pound price of your favorite cold cereal with the per-pound price of potatoes, flour, day-old bread, and even eggs. By adding variety to your breakfasts, you can save significant amounts of money! Some of the cheap breakfast items you might try are muffins, potato pancakes, fried corn loaf, French toast, pancakes, and one-eyed Egyptian sandwiches. Check the recipes.

Cold cereal is an expensive habit.

Occasionally, cereal is a good buy for non-breakfast use. Oatmeal is a good extender in meat loaf. It doesn't "show-up" as readily as crackers or bread crumbs and is especially nourishing. Corn flake crumbs—the kind made with corn flakes and a rolling pin, *not* the kind sold pre-crushed in a box—make excellent crispy breading for oven-fried chicken, but a flour dredging will be a good deal cheaper.

Flour and Grains

Buying flour in bulk may present a storage problem that counter-top canisters just can't deal with. But if you can store it, a bulk purchase can provide a substantial saving. The large pickle jars from restaurants or delicatessens can help out here. If you have room in your freezer, that's the ideal place to store bulk quantities of flour. Whole wheat flour in particular should be frozen or refrigerated if stored for extended periods because it spoils faster than white flour.

Cornmeal is due for a comeback.

Cornmeal is a healthful and versatile grain staple, unless there are corn allergies in your household. Fewer menus include its use than in early pioneer days, but there are some wonderful choices—spoon bread, muffins, Indian pudding, and that standby with the unfortunate moniker, cornmeal mush.

Beans, rice, lentils, and barley are inexpensive and serve as dietary mainstays in many cultures. By using a variety of grains (rice and barley) and legumes (peas, beans, and lentils), you are providing complete protein nutrition without using meat. All of these are good in casseroles, soups, or in side dishes. A pressure cooker can cut the preparation time as well as the amount of energy needed for cooking.

Grains are a dietary bargain!

Get into the habit of adding your own spices to the meals you cook. When spices have been added at the factory to make a convenience food, you can pay double the price or more. A 12-ounce box of River Brand rice (69¢) plus an onion (12¢) and a pinch of oregano (5¢) will cost considerably less than a 10-ounce "gourmet" rice mix for $1.39.

Add your own spices.

Beware the rice-plus-pasta mixes—they are less nutritious than a good brown rice alone, and they're loaded with chemicals. Furthermore, a box that *looks* about the same size as a box of plain rice might weigh only half as much. Check the unit pricing and compare with plain rice or pasta!

Rice can be nutritionally rich, or just empty calories—depending on what the rice company does to it. "Minute Rice," for example, should be pronounced with the accent on the second syllable. It has a minute (my-nyoot) amount of food value left after processing. Plain brown rice costs less and has more food value. Co-ops often offer rice at bargain prices.

46

I used instant rice for years because I couldn't make the uncooked kind come out right. I also spent a lot more money than I needed to. Check the recipe section for a fool-proof method for cooking rice. The oven method, if you're already heating something else, is especially easy.

About Dairy Products

When buying dairy products at the grocery store, it's easy to spend a lot of money without realizing it. Most of us are pretty cautious about the prices we pay for milk, cheese, eggs, and margarine. But it's easy to get carried away with cottage cheese, yogurt, chip dip, sour cream, buttermilk, and ice cream.

From a health and price standpoint, when you buy milk, the best advice is to buy skim. A common fallacy is that 2 percent milk is practically fat-free. It's not. Whole milk has a fat content of 3.25 percent or more. If you want to avoid fat, use skim or nonfat dry milk.

A few years ago it was much cheaper to use nonfat dry milk for all your cooking, and I was a die-hard "cook only with dry milk" fan. Of late, however, this is not the case. Imagine my surprise when I figured out that using powdered milk is *more* costly than buying whole liquid milk! Maybe this surprises you, too, but I have checked several stores in a couple of states and I assure you, nonfat dry milk is not cheaper than whole milk. In some cases it's downright expensive.

This might be a temporary phenomenon. By all logic, dry milk should cost less. Farmers get paid less for it than for fluid milk, and the processors and stores don't have to keep it refrigerated. So watch the prices. If the prices go down, keep in mind that even if your kids don't like to drink it, dry milk is every bit as good, and more convenient, than whole milk for cooking.

Leftover rice with brown sugar and milk makes a fine breakfast cereal for about 10¢ a serving.

Although it used to be cheaper, at this writing, dry milk is more expensive than fresh milk!

47

Even at a slightly higher price, there are some excellent reasons for using dry milk. For one thing, it doesn't require any special handling or refrigeration. It'll just sit on your shelf, month after month, minding its own business until one day when the refrigerator breaks down or you get laid off at work. Another reason for having dry milk on hand is that it truly has no fat. Also, dry milk is a good way of getting an extra wallop of calcium in your diet—dump some in with other dry ingredients when you're baking, and you'll never know it's there. Finally, some things are easier to make using dry milk. For instance, if you are thickening a gravy with flour, mix dry milk with the flour before adding the liquid—that almost guarantees you'll have no lumps. But remember, it's still not cheaper, at least at this writing.

Delivered dairy products are expensive. When I had a charge account with the dairy I got carried away *very* quickly. It's *so* tempting to take the dairy up on its offer to help you wake up to heavy cream in your coffee. And if toasted almond fudge ice cream is on sale this month, who among us could resist? I learned my lesson. I now confine my purchases to the store.

Processed cheeses, including pasteurized processed cheese, cheese food, cheese spreads, cold-pack cheese food, and club cheese, are made with blends of natural cheeses that are shredded and mixed with other ingredients. Some of the ingredients are for texture, some are for flavor and color, and some are preservatives to extend the shelf-life of the products. Because of the chemicals, many people prefer natural cheese—even though processed cheeses are less expensive, melt easily, and are convenient for grilled cheese sandwiches, cheeseburgers, casseroles, and sauces.

Never throw out bits of cheese just because they've gotten hard.

> If you want to slice cheese with a knife, wet the knife between cutting slices to prevent sticking. Or use an adjustable cheese slicer. It cuts slices with a wire, and the slices are a uniform thickness. This tends to keep the kids from cutting slices of odd dimensions and leaving a strange-looking piece that cannot be sliced.

Cheese is very nutritious and versatile, although high in cholesterol. It isn't cheap, but you can do so much with it and stretch it so far that it can still be a good buy. Cheese can be refrigerated or frozen, so large quantities can be purchased when on sale.

I led the home economist at our county extension office on a merry chase when I called to ask if cottage cheese (incredibly high in protein and relatively low in cholesterol) can be safely frozen. After checking several books that she had, and a couple that she borrowed, she found that it *can* be frozen. Having tried it, though, I will tell you that the quality leaves something to be desired—the curds become dry and crumbly! If you can find it on sale, you might want to give it a try, though. You may not want to eat it straight, but you can use it as a cheaper substitute for ricotta in cooking Italian dishes.

Even if you don't like the taste, cottage cheese can be used as a hidden protein in many dishes.

Yogurt can be substituted for sour cream, and some people like the taste in low-calorie salad dressings. It adds a distinctive "tang." Some folks buy yogurt thinking that they're saving a lot of calories. If, however, you note the calories listed on any eight-ounce container of fruit yogurt, you'll find that it's in the 220-240 calorie range. That's not as "lo-cal" as some of us might like to think. However, everything is relative. Compared

Homemade yogurt is ridiculously easy to make.

And cheap!

to the number of calories in an equal amount of sour cream (720), it's a substantial saving.

Many of the calories in fruit yogurt come from the fruit mixture, which (before mixing into the yogurt) is very similar to canned pie filling. It's very high in sugar. You might want to consider adding fresh fruit, vanilla, instant coffee powder, or pureed baby food to plain yogurt instead of buying fruit yogurt. Apple sauce mixed with plain yogurt is delicious. My favorite is "breakfast yogurt," with fruit, chopped nuts, and a little puffed cereal or granola.

The cheapest yogurt is homemade. The only ingredients are milk and half a teaspoon of starter per pint. You can salvage the starter from the last batch of yogurt. If milk is $1 for a half-gallon, then plain yogurt will cost about 12½¢ per eight-ounce serving (versus 50¢ or more for individual, store-bought cups that you can't recycle). If nature or a neighbor gives you free berries to add, you have a cheap and nutritious breakfast or snack. Blending it with fruit, sugar if desired, and unflavored gelatin will make incredible "ice cream" bars.

As far as ice cream goes, almost any kid under the age of 12, and a great many older ones, can be fooled into eating ice milk or sherbet, with less fat and less cost than ice cream. (It's what a lot of frozen custard stands sell for ice cream.) You can make a very passable substitute with frozen flavored gelatin whipped, re-frozen, re-whipped, and frozen a third time. It's so cheap it's silly. Refreeze promptly.

Then there are homemade frozen pops. You can buy little pop makers with handles on the sticks, or use crafts sticks. Freeze juice, lemonade, or good pudding.

Another hint—freeze lemonade or iced tea in ice cube trays and use the cubes in iced tea. It won't water down like ice cubes, and costs very little. For a party, just put a cherry or mint leaf in each cube—pretty, special, and cheap.

Whipped cream is expensive—the only way to save money on whipped cream is by not serving it. A lower-cost substitute can be made from evaporated milk, with vanilla and sweetening added. Freeze it, whip it, refreeze, rewhip, then freeze again. Or you could buy a topping mix that uses just a little milk and vanilla (and maybe some chemicals).

Fancy frozen treats needn't be expensive.

Snack food

One reason not to take the kids to the grocery store with you is the pleading you'll get to buy a commercially prepared snack that has been widely touted on TV. Most of these have little or no nutritional value, at a huge cost to your food budget!

Popcorn is probably the best snack you can buy (or grow). It's cheap, low in calories, and healthful. There are white and yellow varieties of popcorn. The white is hull-less and pops up smaller than the yellow. The taste is also a little different.

To make sure that popcorn is good to the last pop, keep kernels in the refrigerator.

I keep popcorn in a closed jar or bag in the refrigerator. It has to maintain a 12% moisture content to make enough steam when heated to explode the kernel. In my experience, the only difference between "gourmet" popcorn and "cheap" popcorn is the price.

Making cookies and bread pretzels are projects that kids can enjoy doing themselves. Some of the no-bake recipes are especially appropriate for young children. And finger gelatin is just plain fun for anyone. (Check the recipe section.)

About Spices

One terrific way to save money is by using spices to make cheaper cuts of meat or other "plain" foods more flavorful and appealing. (After all, that's what Christopher Columbus was looking for back in 1492.) My favorites are cinnamon, ginger, clove, bay leaf, tarragon, garlic, cayenne, oregano, dill, and, of course, salt and pepper. Spices frequently are not cheap, but they add so much and stretch so far that they are a worthwhile investment. Try to find a wholesale vendor or co-op. The difference in price is surprising.

Cheap food doesn't have to taste terrible.

This is also an area where gardening makes sense. You can grow chili peppers just about anywhere in the United States, and the harvest from half a dozen plants, dried and ground into powder, can make up a healthy little jar of unadulterated hot stuff. Garlic is also easy to grow. Simply split a bulb into all its natural little parts (cloves) and plant, indoors or out. Then when you are seasoning, you can use the green parts of the plant, too.

Even if you don't think of yourself as a gardener, you can grow garlic in a pot.

I almost never buy spices that are mixed with salt (e.g., onion salt or garlic salt). They're usually cheaper than an equal-sized container of pure garlic or onion powder, and they should be—salt is cheap. I don't always want salt with my garlic, but if I do, the powder goes a lot further if I add the salt. I do buy "lemon pepper" on occasion. It's terrific on beef or chicken. Usually, however, spice blends are much more expensive than single spices. I mix my own.

About Nonfood Items

It is an unfortunate comment on our society that a trip to the food store often costs more for nonfood items—paper goods, cleaning supplies, pet foods, and (perish the thought) tobacco and alcohol—than for edibles.

How often have you said, "There must be some way to save on these things that we can't even eat." Well, there is. There's always a way to save somewhere.

One way to cut spending is to avoid disposables. If you can throw it away, chances are you'll just have to buy it again later, and you can bet the price will be up the next time. I almost never buy paper towels, paper napkins, paper cups, disposable flatware, paper or plastic plates. (Okay, maybe once a year for a picnic reunion, I can justify buying throwaways. But any regular use is just too costly.) Enamelled tinware, when you can find it, is fairly inexpensive. It's the perfect answer for a picnic or barbecue.

Throw-aways are almost always wasteful.

If you have a baby, you might give some thought to cloth diapers. You can hire a diaper service for about the same cost as disposable diapers, or save a lot of money by washing them yourself. The environmental impact is often debated. But I personally find it hard to believe that washing diapers is anywhere near as harmful as filling the landfills with tons of poo-filled plastic.

Toilet Paper

There are some disposables that you can't get along without. Things like toilet paper.

As with foods, the generic brands of toilet paper deserve to be tried. If they are not satisfactory, they should be rejected in favor of the next cheapest brand, until you find the lowest-cost brand that is satisfactory to your family. (One friend describes generic toilet paper as John Wayne toilet paper: It's rough, tough, and won't take anything off anybody.)

Would you buy toilet paper from John Wayne?

Buying name-brand toilet paper in large quantities is sometimes cheap, and our warehouse-type store has it by the case at a dramatic saving.

A key issue in determining value in toilet paper is the number of sheets per roll. Often, the cheaper rolls contain fewer sheets, but they're fluffed up with air to look like more. If a name brand costs slightly more, but offers double the coverage, it's a better deal. In my experience, Scott Tissue lasts a lot longer on the roller than generic or house brands. But when the generic and house-brand companies emulate Scott, with huge numbers of sheets per roll, they may offer prices that are even more favorable.

Compare the price per sheet, not per roll.

Cleaning Supplies

The cost of cleaning supplies can be reduced if you consolidate. There is no reason to use one cleaner for the basin, another for the toilet bowl, and another for the shower stall. My cleaning basket contains an all-purpose cleanser (usually Murphy's Oil Soap), scouring cleanser, chlorine bleach, ammonia, a small bottle of furniture polish (*not* a spray can—aerosols are expensive), a spot remover, and a few rags. I also have baking soda, vinegar, and dish-washing liquid.

Vinegar is the most versatile of cheap cleaners.

Sound too simple? There isn't anything I can't clean with it. Okay, I'm sure that a collection of old spoons or antique lace or something might require a special cleaner, but by and large, this will do.

The bleach will disinfect anything that gets germy, and the ammonia takes care of all glass. Some people use just vinegar and newspapers on glass with fine results and no tears. Some commercial window cleaners advertise that they come with "real vinegar" or "with ammonia." Well, vinegar and ammonia are cheap. Why not buy them alone and skip the coloring and perfume?

I pay 59¢ for a quart of vinegar, which I then dilute with three parts water. Put this in a pump sprayer (cost: about $2, a one-time expense) and there you have it. By contrast, commercial window cleaner costs about $3.

When I worked in the fast-food industry, the procedure for cleaning the rest rooms was to pour chlorine bleach into the toilet bowls and then clean the seats and the top of the toilet with a spray cleaner containing ammonia. Even the small amount of ammonia mixed with the bleach in the toilet bowl produced fumes which caused burning eyes and coughing.

> *Note: Never mix chlorine bleach with ammonia or any product that contains ammonia. Doing so creates a gas that can cause serious injury or death!!!*

Ammonia is good for cleaning ovens. A small dish of ammonia in the oven overnight will loosen anything baked on, so no scrubbing is necessary. A little ammonia and a piece of tin foil in the dish water will clean silverware. Just be sure to triple rinse—ammonia is a poison.

I do *not* use ammonia to mop floors; it removes floor wax and, if you have a puppy, it encourages accidents. I never clean up pet stains with ammonia (or any product containing ammonia) for the same reason. On the other hand, it does make a dandy paper-training aid. A few drops of ammonia on the newspaper will beckon to a puppy and tell him that this is clearly *the* place to be.

Use ammonia to paper-train your pup.

Pet stains clean up nicely with white vinegar and water, mixed half and half. The oil soap in my cleaning basket will wash anything, including furniture and fine washable clothing, and, as a matter of fact, dish-washing liquid could probably be left out entirely if I wanted to use oil soap on my dishes. It is safe and effective, but it makes wet dishes a little too slippery for comfort. I use spot remover sparingly for the sake of my upholstery and my budget.

I use scouring cleanser for bathroom fixtures, pots, and pans. I use baking soda to scour the insides of my refrigerator and the counter tops. I also set an open box inside to absorb odors. In a solution, I use baking soda to sweeten thermos bottles. Vinegar, too, will kill odors. Just set some out in a saucer, and nasty odors disappear.

Baking soda in the dishwasher cuts spotting.

I'm experimenting with ways to cut down on the price of dishwasher compound. I use the biggest box of house-brand or generic dishwasher soap, and wash only when the dishwasher is full. I don't fill the little soap cups quite full, though, and the dishes seem to get just as clean.

If you have a fiberglass or plastic bathtub, you should avoid scouring cleansers. Even the "soft scrub" varieties may damage the finish. Yet ordinary, non-abrasive cleaners will not restore the shiny, clean finish. Try vinegar.

Yet another use for vinegar!

By the way, don't invest in commercial copper cleaner. Instead, mix about two tablespoons of vinegar with a tablespoon of salt. Brush it on with a paint brush or a rag and rinse off promptly. Voila! Clean copper, cheap!

Laundry

Saving money in the laundry is easy, if you measure everything you use and avoid unnecessary additives, such as de-greasers, de-spotters, and fabric softeners. Some folks use "dryer sheets" of fabric softener. I buy the cheapest I can find, then cut each sheet in half, and use each half twice. If your water is "hard," you can use half a cup of vinegar in the wash water and skip the softener.

Make sure you're not doing the same job twice. If your fabric softener whitens, you shouldn't need a whitening agent, and if your detergent has bleach, maybe you won't have to add any more. Keep it simple. The fewer products you buy, the less money you spend, the less you will pollute the environment, and the less time you will waste running back and forth to the laundry room.

Use a small amount of boiling water to get out certain stains such as grape juice. For grease spots, try rubbing in a bit of shampoo or dishwasher soap. Then wash the full load with cold water. It'll get just as clean.

Remember, no dumping allowed!

Liquid detergent dissolves better in cold water than does powdered detergent. If your best buy is a granulated one, dissolve it in a cup of warm water first—then use cold water for washing.

Although it takes more time, drying your laundry on a clothesline is a *huge* energy saver. While towels might not feel quite as fluffy, the brisk scrub and fresh smell are energizing! If you do use a dryer, you can vent it indoors with a water-filled lint trap. There's no point in wasting the heat, if the weather is the least bit chilly, unless you have an extremely tight house that is vulnerable to moisture damage.

Toilet Articles

Another big expense may be toilet articles. Spray deodorant is invariably more expensive per ounce than stick or roll on. To cut costs, you might try a powdering of baking soda.

Baking soda mixed with cornstarch is a good deodorant "powder"— add a little perfume, if you like.

Vinegar on your hair after shampooing can replace cream rinse or conditioner. But experiment with some care—some people swear by these low-cost substitutes, while others swear at them. These may act as a bleach which can turn hair streaky and may not be good for dry hair.

There are natural rinses you can make at home as well. For brunettes, steep two tablespoons of rosemary or sage in one cup hot water for one hour and use as a rinse. Steep two tablespoons of chamomile in lemon juice to make a rinse for blondes.

Just because one person needs expensive dandruff shampoo doesn't mean the whole family should use it.

Try a different brand of baby shampoo if that's what you use. Most stores carry their own brands, and these tend to be very much like national brands. If shampoo is just soap to you, investigate buying it at some of the discount houses. Some of these carry shampoo in half-gallon bottles for real savings. I have a friend who buys half gallons of shampoo at a discount house, and because the shampoo is very thick, mixes it half-and-half with water. She doubles her savings and her hip-length hair is beautiful.

Another acquaintance, whose kids are fussy about using brand-name products, buys cheap shampoo in big jugs, and refills the name-brand bottles when the kids aren't looking. Cheap dandruff shampoos don't always work as well as expensive brands, but they deserve to be tried.

Tooth-powder for pennies!

You can save money by using baking soda (mixed with salt) instead of toothpaste. Not only is it a good treatment to keep your gums healthy, it even gets rid of coffee and tobacco stains, I'm told!

To use up soap scraps, sew two wash cloths together on three sides and put snaps on the fourth. Presto! A self-soaping wash mitt!

58

Pets

Finally, we come to the one member of the family for whom you don't have to cook—the family pet. This doesn't mean that you're off the hook. Pets are often fussy eaters. If I try to feed plain dry food to my dog, she just eats around the meal and "starves" dramatically until I give in and give her what she wants.

Maybe you're strong and can be firm with your pet and save lots of money. Good luck. Friends of ours owned three beautiful collies who ate better than most people I know.

What to do? One answer is to get a smaller pet. The amount of money you spend feeding your pet is in direct proportion to its size. A pug eats less than a great dane. A goldfish eats less than that. (Of course, you can pamper fish as well. Mine feel absolutely deserted unless I give them a periodic offering of brine shrimp and, believe it or not, canned spinach. Sharks love spinach. Just a little out of the can, mashed as it is with no butter or seasoning, and they're thrilled. Okay, I know I'm not the best role-model for feeding pets cheaply, but I'm working on it!)

Watch for sales at the discount chain stores.

If you have a new pet—a new puppy or kitten from the pound, for example—introduce it to cheap eating. Pets, like people, insist on the foods that they are used to. If you treat them to fancy canned food early in life, that will become their preference. If you introduce them to cheap, dried food instead, they will be satisfied, knowing there'll be table scraps now and then. If your pets are not getting enough scraps from your house, scrounge around. Dried food alone is not enough for most dogs and cats.

Pets develop their tastes early in life.

Buy Nonfood Items at Other Stores

Supermarkets are often (not always) the best places to buy food. They generally are *not* the best places to buy other commodities. They offer other items because people like the convenience of making all their purchases during the weekly grocery shopping. Some supermarkets even sell lawn mowers. As long as people are willing to pay for that type of convenience, the supermarkets will offer it.

Sometimes, the convenience of buying nonfood items at the supermarket is worthwhile. If you desperately need a couple of light bulbs, and the nearest home store or discount store is several miles away, it might make sense to pick them up during grocery shopping. But if you're stocking up, find a store that sells light bulbs at a lower price.

Department stores, discount stores, and home stores have a better variety of most non-food items, at lower cost, than do supermarkets. Examples include kitchen utensils, cleaning supplies, vacuum-cleaner bags, motor oil, and snow shovels. They may also have lower prices on laundry detergent, shampoo, deodorants, aspirin, and a long list of other items that supermarkets offer. Some even offer beverages and specific foods at bargain prices. You may not visit these other stores as often, but when you do, stock up, so that the inflated supermarket prices won't add to your grocery bill.

Most people love to give advice—just ask "Where's the cheapest place to buy . . ."

When light bulbs are on sale at eight for $1, stock up with a five-year supply!

Chapter 5
Buying in Bulk

The smaller the package, the more you're paying for what's inside. If you want to start saving money, you have to think big. In food, that means buying in bulk. Trying to buy meat in bulk can be a little like buying a car. You have to know what you're talking about, shop around, and haggle fearlessly.

Beef

Learning the language is the first step. The price quoted is "hanging weight," and this includes bone and fat. Since you probably won't want to take home bone and fat, the butcher will dispose of it for you. Therefore, although you may be paying $1 per pound, you won't be taking home a full pound of meat for each dollar you pay. (But you'll still be coming out ahead.)

The way to determine how much waste you will have is by the "yield grade." This is a code, from Y-1 to Y-5. Y-1 has the least waste, Y-5 the most. Y-3 is about average, and includes about one-third waste.

You will almost always be paying extra for cutting, wrapping, and freezing. This may cost around 10¢ per pound. If you are buying a side of Y-3 beef—say, 300 pounds—at $1 per pound plus 10¢ per pound processing, you can expect to receive 200 pounds of beef. Your actual cost is $330 divided by 200 pounds, or $1.65 per pound. I don't know if that sounds high for ground beef, but it's pretty darn good for porterhouse steak.

By buying a "side" you can get steaks and roasts for the price of good hamburger.

**It won't be
all steaks.**

**Do you have
any idea how
big half a
steer is?**

The meat processor will ask you how you want
the meat cut up. If you aren't prepared for it,
this question can throw you. It's okay to ask for
suggestions, but it will help to know that the
flank and brisket are usually ground or cubed.
The steaks and roasts come from around the
center back. The front quarter is tougher, and
costs less per pound if bought separately.

Some folks buy a side of beef and have it all
made into ground beef. I would never do that
unless I had been snookered into buying meat
that was too tough or dry to be cooked any other
way. To grind steaks or roasts into "hamburger"
seems somehow disrespectful and deprives you of
going to the freezer when the need for something
special arises. More important, ground beef
shouldn't be frozen for more than three or four
months. It takes a sturdy constitution to polish
off 200 pounds of ground beef in three months.

It's important to shop around for a major
meat purchase. Check with grocers, butchers, and
beef or pork farmers. Find out the cost per
pound and yield grade. Discuss the price the
competition offered, if it's lower. (Don't fib. The
competitors in this business may be friends, and
you may be left red-faced if you are less than
totally honest.) Ask how much extra processing
costs. Ask if it includes freezing. It can take two
or three days to freeze 200 pounds of beef cuts
in your freezer, adding to your electric bill.

Be certain you have enough room in your
freezer before you order. Half a cow will not fit
into a basic kitchen refrigerator-freezer. If you
don't have a freezer of sufficient size, it's often
possible to rent a frozen food locker for a few
dollars a month. These are not always pleasant
places. Their locations often resemble a room full
of long file cabinet drawers, freezing to walk into,
slippery, and sometimes smelling like a meat-

processing plant. The cost, however, is comparable to the cost of electricity to run a freezer at home, without the cost of buying one.

If you buy a freezer, keep in mind that a chest-type freezer is more energy-efficient than an upright freezer. You can improve energy efficiency if you put the freezer in a cool part of the house—ideally, in an unheated room or cold pantry. That will hold down the costs considerably, at least during the winter months.

Always try to look at your meat before buying. (It will look like a skinned, dead animal. If this bothers you, skip it.) With beef, look for fat. There should be some. If the processor tells you, "It's better with no fat," look for another butcher. It happened that we almost got taken by a "bait-and-switch" meat processor with no-fat beef. Wisdom (or suspicion) won out and we left meatless. An acquaintance, however, wasn't so lucky and wound up grinding $250 worth of nearly inedible beef.

A "cheap" upright freezer may cost a fortune to operate.

If you're not careful, you could end up with 200 lbs. of shoe leather.

Pork

A half hog will probably weigh about 80 to 100 pounds, but weights can vary a lot. A "split half hog" may *not* be half a hog. It's usually a quarter of a hog, split lengthwise. Frequently, meat processors will offer specials if you buy meat in bulk, and a split half hog is a favorite. It is about 40 pounds, hanging weight. If you figure on losing a third to waste, you'll be getting about 25-30 pounds of pork. This may be 25-30 pounds of pork sections bearing no relation to each other (such as ham or chops) and it may be smoked or fresh. This may or may not be a good deal. Be suspicious. Find out which cuts will be included in your split half hog, and whether they're smoked or fresh.

Another come-on is to give away several chickens with a meat order. If you have a use for several tough whole stewing chickens, this might be an incentive, if you plan to buy anyway. If you don't need stewing chickens, and you aren't totally comfortable with the quality of the meat you will be buying, don't buy. You can buy a great many lovely fryers for the money you'll waste on a bad side or quarter of meat.

Buyer beware!

Specials

There are times when you can buy meat specials at department stores, in shopping malls, and at roadside refrigerated trucks. These are usually "portion-controlled" meats. This means that a six-ounce or eight-ounce steak weighs exactly six or eight ounces. Often this is done by chopping and forming beef, chicken, fish, or shrimp into a particular size and shape to make it look like it came that way. (This often is done with pork.) Your clue to portion-controlled meat sales is a sign or an ad that states a quantity of steaks for a set price (20 for $19.95, for example). If you are buying regular meats, the price is almost never set by count because of the near impossibility of cutting steaks of equal weights.

Meat specials may be highly processed food, some with filler added.

Portion-controlled meats are fine to eat, though hardly of gourmet quality. The texture is different from that of a regular steak. They're almost never tough, but that's because they may have been chemically tenderized. Many restaurants use portion-controlled meats. They're handy, and generally inexpensive to buy.

Many groceries and butchers have specialty meat packages that may include a variety of beef, pork, poultry, or fish cuts. I have used them with great satisfaction. (I'm lucky enough to have a trustworthy butcher.) It's useful to buy a month's supply of meat with one phone call. These packages, however, are not always cheaper. If your butcher doesn't have available the approximate weight of the package, the cost per pound, and the total cost, skip the package and buy meats separately. It takes longer, but it may be safer and cheaper.

Certain food plans can be purchased that allow you to order not only meats, but all kinds of frozen foods, delivered to you on a regular schedule. If you don't own a freezer, they will throw one into the deal (for a nominal monthly fee, of course). It's convenient and probably fairly dependable.

Your own frozen food plan is probably the best bet if you shop carefully.

If you are house-bound, it may be worth the extra expense. But don't be fooled into thinking this is an inexpensive way to buy food. It isn't. I have a friend who called to investigate buying food from a frozen food plan. It bothered her that no matter how she tried, the salesman wouldn't give her a price per pound, ounce, or serving. Not only that, the plan would have cost her 85-90 percent of her food budget without allowing for fresh fruits and vegetables, dairy products, toiletries, and cleaning supplies. There is one way of saving money on a frozen food plan—by becoming a salesperson, you might get a discount!

If the unit prices are a guarded secret, you can bet it's not a good deal.

Buying Fruits and Vegetables in Bulk

When purchasing fruits and vegetables in bulk, consider what types of produce you need, and what is in season. Define what constitutes "bulk" for your needs.

For example, if you live alone and want to make a little tomato juice, a couple of pecks of juice tomatoes will do fine. If, however, you need tomato sauce for six months for a family of five, you might do better with a couple of bushels of sauce tomatoes instead.

I always consider the method I plan to use for preserving (see chapter seven). If I plan to can, I don't wait until late August or September to buy canning jars and lids. By that time they might not be in the stores. If I plan to freeze, I decide on either freezer boxes or bags. When I choose boxes, I try to get them in advance. Other things that may come into short supply are sugar, pectin, and rubber jar rings.

Nothing can ruin your evening as surely as having a gallon of bubbling grape jelly on the stove, ready to put into sterilized jars, with no lids to seal it. Having tried to find paraffin for sealing jelly at 10:30 p.m., I can assure you that being prepared is rule number one in my kitchen.

Places to check for bulk produce are grocery stores, farms, roadside stands, and friends or acquaintances who may have a bumper crop that they are unable to use. Another place to check is grocery wholesalers.

Vegetables such as beans, peas, potatoes, carrots, tomatoes, onions, and brussels sprouts are usually sold by volume—a peck or a bushel. But corn, melons, winter squash, cabbage, celery, head lettuce, and pumpkins may be sold by count or by pound. Fruit—oranges, grapefruit, apples, and pears—are sold by the peck or bushel, with an estimated count. If the prices are by count only, you may not be getting bulk prices.

Where to Buy

Your grocer will be happy to sell produce to you in bulk, but don't imagine that you'll be paying wholesale. The grocer buys the produce wholesale, and has to mark it up regardless of the price he or she charges you. The grocer can't stay in business without making a profit on each transaction. Any time you pay a middleman, you pay more.

If your only choice for bulk produce is a grocer, don't go in and buy from the refrigerated bins. Contact the produce manager or the store manager. Explain what you are looking for and how much you need. Many produce managers will be able to help you avoid costly mistakes. Sometimes they will order extra of what you want. Be sure to get a price quote before you order—something more exact than "probably a few bucks." Be sure to stipulate your right of refusal of any produce that is of poor quality, or other than what you agreed to. Then don't be afraid to refuse it if necessary.

Avoid middlemen when possible.

This is not to say that you should refuse delivery if you spot a few bad apples. As with meat, there will always be some waste on any large delivery of produce, and one of the trade-offs in paying wholesale prices is that you lose the right to sort through piece-by-piece. It's a question of proportion. If you throw away half a bushel of carrots, you will have to buy twice as many to get what you need. That could wipe out any saving.

Farmers' markets vary greatly. Some of the best ones are damp, drafty, and cheap. Other farmers' markets are glossy, glitzy, cute, and expensive. They cater to tourists and gourmet shoppers. Going to a true farmers' market, one with piles and crates of fruits and vegetables, is an adventure. In some places, be prepared to haggle. And be prepared to stand, carry, and be damp (many are outside). It takes time and patience to get the best buys. Shopping near closing time is a good way to save some money, if you don't mind having less selection.

It doesn't take many bananas to make ten loaves of banana bread, which is about all you can mix in a wash basin at one time!

An even better way to purchase bulk vegetables and fruits is to buy directly from the farmer. This can be done in several ways. One is to contact farmers you know and buy directly from them.

67

If you don't know any farmers, watch for produce signs during a drive to the country, or check newspaper ads. Call ahead if possible, to negotiate a price.

Now we arrive at what may be an exciting adventure or a pain in the rear: pick-your-own farms. You simply take your baskets out to a farm that grows what you want to buy, and pick as much as you want. Simple, right? Not always. If you aren't familiar with farms, you might want to bear a few things in mind.

Remember to take your own container so you don't end up paying extra for one.

Lesson one. Picking lots of anything can be hard work. Think about it. Crops grow in dirt, with the help of manure, rain, and sun. Some are pollinated by bees and other insects. Where there are insects, there also may be creatures that live on insects, including snakes. Then there is the sunburn.

All this is in addition to the sheer effort involved. If you decide to use a pick-your-own farm, and you pick two or three bushels of green beans, are you going to be out of commission for three days recovering? Fresh produce must be processed right away, and that can be a tiring job by itself. If all this sounds overwhelming, leave the picking to someone else.

Plan to get your hands dirty.

If you do decide that picking your own is for you, plan to get dirty. Take extra shoes. Take newspaper to line your trunk or the back of your station wagon. If you're driving an open truck, you may want to cover your purchases to keep the sun off them during the trip home. Wear gardening gloves. If there are known to be poisonous snakes in the area, wear high boots. (Chances are that any snakes are going to slither off as soon as they hear you coming, but it makes sense to be on the safe side.)

68

PICK YOUR
OWN
APPLES
Rhutabaga
Strawberries

Don't forget the sun block!

Wear sun block and don't forget to cover your lips. Sun poisoning makes a sunburn feel good by comparison. One very fair young lady I know used sun block everywhere except her lips, got a nasty case of sun poisoning that caused her to miss three days of work, pile up a stack of doctor's bills, and eat all her meals through a straw for two weeks. That's not a way to save money.

Finally, set a time limit on your work—say, about two hours. Take along a thermos of iced tea, lemonade, or water, and rest frequently. Try to schedule your foray for early morning or late afternoon, to avoid the worst of the heat. If, after your set time has elapsed, you still want to go on, quit anyway, and come back later. Saving money should not create a hardship.

People who run pick-your-own farms must be saints to put up with the little kids who eat more than they pack.

If you have small children, you might want to plan a short outing to enjoy a day at the farm—apart from any economy measures. It's an educational adventure for kids that can be a lot of fun if you're not feeling harried by having to show a certain amount for your labors.

Just because it's touted as farm fresh or "bulk" doesn't mean it's always less expensive than what you can find at the supermarket. If you're picking it, it's in season, which probably means that it's also on sale at the supermarket. That it's cheap compared to what you paid last winter is irrelevant. Don't work your knuckles white without comparing current prices first.

Compare pick-it prices with the supermarket ones.

I've tried to cover the negative aspects of bulk buying and picking, simply because first-timers rarely know what to expect. If I haven't scared you off, you'll probably find it to be a delightful, money-saving experience and quality time with any who share the adventure!

Chapter 6
Growing Your Own

Some of the absolutely cheapest foods are those that you can grow in your garden. For the price of a few packets of seeds, you can feed a family for a year or more. Of course, as with most things that cost less, you have to work for it; but there is no more satisfying feeling in the world than eating food you have grown yourself.

For years, we planted a 50- by 100-foot garden. We planted sweet corn, popcorn, cucumbers, winter squash, three kinds of tomatoes, green bell peppers, green beans, yellow wax beans, sugar snap peas, cantaloupe, watermelon, cabbage, brussels sprouts, lettuce, eggplant, onions, carrots, radishes, and potatoes. We dried beans and popcorn, and our squash averaged 32 pounds each. We ate for a year from our harvest and still had tons (perhaps an exaggeration, but it seemed like tons) to give away.

My point is that you can get a remarkable amount of food from a small space, but you need to plan. Maybe 5,000 square feet of garden sounds huge to you. It felt huge to us sometimes. Bear in mind, though, that we grew everything we could think of. (We tend to run to excess in our family. We watched T.V. by kerosene light one entire summer to save money on the electricity bill. After buying kerosene, we probably realized a profit of $1.50.)

It is not necessary for you to plant a huge garden to realize a large saving. If you're strapped for time, you can still get a large har-

It's not necessary to have a large garden to save money.

If you've never tried gardening before, start small—so you won't lose your enthusiasm.

71

**Take time
for careful
planning.**

**Tending a
garden is a
great fitness
plan—and
it's cheaper
than a
Nautilus
workout!**

vest by planting such easy-to-grow vegetables as tomatoes, squash, peppers, and cucumbers. If you live in an apartment and have no gardening space, you can even grow some things in pots.

Be realistic. Are you prepared to devote one to two hours of work, several days a week, to your garden? A large garden with a wide variety of plants can easily require this much effort.

Before starting, you'll need to calculate the approximate yields. One way to do this is to consult the seed packages. They sometimes tell you about how much you can expect to harvest from one package of seeds or one "foot-row." (These yields are, unfortunately, very approximate and depend to a large extent on soil and weather conditions.)

Another place to check is with your cooperative extension service. This government agency answers any question you have on subjects such as gardening, insect pests, and livestock.

Once you know what you want to plant and approximately what yield to expect, stop and refuse to make any additional immediate decisions. This is a crucial time, the point at which there is the greatest danger of either throwing down your pencil in disgust or charging off, eyes glazed, to the feed and seed store to spend $400 on useless gardening paraphernalia.

Have a cup of coffee, read the paper, and go out calmly to look at your proposed garden space. Are you certain that this is the size garden you want to deal with? Are you absolutely positive that you can handle the explosion of produce come next summer? Will you swear that you have the time and will to take care of your plants?

Good. Now cut your plan in half. Why? There are two truths with which you must be familiar before you can start working the soil.

Truth #1: Gardening is hard work.

Truth #2: Gardening can save you money, but it can also lead to temptation to spend large amounts of money unnecessarily.

What You'll Need

If you decide to go ahead, because you're strong and healthy and love working outdoors, great. (It's possible, though unlikely, that you've underestimated how much you can cope with this year. Don't worry—you can always expand the garden next year.) Now you begin to think about the tools of the trade. *Buy only what you absolutely, positively, have to have.*

Think about it. People have been growing things for thousands of years, *without* the cute little gardening hats, kneeling pads, mean little scarecrows for the birds to roost on, or any of the other exciting things that are available.

On the other hand, there are some things that you really should have. Seeds, of course. You'll need a hoe, a spade, and perhaps a garden fork for moving hay and compost. And a way to water the ground (hose or watering can). It's useful to have a small amount of potting soil for some of your plants, and perhaps some aluminum foil to protect new tomato plants from cutworms.

You'll probably need fertilizer, particularly if the patch is new. The best fertilizers are available for free or at low cost in many locations—horse manure or composted kitchen garbage, for example. Costly chemical fertilizers tend to deplete the soil in the long run, and require re-application in larger amounts in future years. In any event, it's a good idea to have your soil tested, or do it yourself with a soil-testing kit.

The garden supply stores and catalogs are full of gadgets and supplies that won't improve your yield, or reduce your labor.

Natural fertilizers are better and cheaper than chemicals.

Try saving seeds instead of buying them. They didn't always come in cute little packets.

If insects are out of control, you might need insecticide. But again, for finances and health, you're better off keeping your garden as natural and organic as possible.

Anything beyond that is surplus. You could buy rolls of black plastic or bark for mulch, to ease the job of weeding. You could buy peat moss, but let's think straight. We are trying to save money here, not appear in *House Beautiful*.

Certain plants such as tomatoes, broccoli, and peppers, which have a long growing season, should be started indoors before spring has arrived. This lets you protect them while they're too young to fend for themselves. You can sprout your seeds in peat pellets that swell to two inches or so when you water them. Unfortunately, you have to pay for each of those little pellets. A cheaper method is to cut a milk carton in half lengthwise, and fill each half with potting soil.

(Some plants, such as carrots, will not survive transplanting. You'll have to sow these directly in the garden. Read seed packets to find what will survive transplanting.)

If you don't have the time or patience to start seedlings in the house, you can buy them at the local nursery, home store, or hardware store. A cost-saving tip: buy them at the end of the "plant-buying" season. After a certain date each spring (the date depends on your local climate), tomato plants, pepper plants, etc., go on sale, at prices next to nothing. That's the time to buy! Your garden harvest may come a little later than your neighbor's. But it will be just as good, and unlike your neighbor, you will have obtained your plants at a bargain price.

The same principle can often apply to seeds. Packets of seeds that cost 65¢ at the beginning of the season may be reduced to 10¢ at the end of the season. The same is true of last year's seeds, if they're still available. They may have only a 50 percent germination rate, but plant twice as many and you'll still save money.

Don't carry this idea to an extreme—gardening is a time-sensitive activity. Planting too late may mean that you won't enjoy the harvest. But you can save money by adjusting your planting cycle to take advantage of sale prices.

Big bargains come to those who wait.

Preparing the Ground

If neither you nor the previous tenant ever kept a garden, chances are slim that you'll have a nice, neat, clear patch of earth to work in. Choose an area that gets at least half a day's sun, preferably more. Mark it off with stakes at each corner and run string between the stakes.

Now comes the hard part. With soil that has not been worked in a long time, preparation for your garden is not going to be easy. Weeds or grass don't want to be uprooted. And just turning them over once isn't going to be good enough. Unless they're buried deep, they'll be back, bullying your vegetables out of the way.

If your garden spot is in the shade, the results will be very disappointing!

The solution is trenching. It's a pain, but fortunately it has to be done only once. The process involves digging off a two-foot length of sod and putting it aside. Then dig down another foot or so, putting that earth aside as well. Finally, next to this hole, dig another two-foot length of sod, throw it in the trench, and put the clean earth on top. By repeating this process throughout the patch, you will have a weed-free (for now) plot with lots of good, nutritious, decaying grass and weeds down deep where they can only help.

An easy solution is a friendly farmer who will disc and harrow your space.

If you're not up to hand-digging, the job can be made easier by renting a good-quality rototiller for a day. But in virgin space, you'll still need to do some shovel work. You might want to

75

hire some teen-age kids to help. The hard work of preparing a garden spot is a one-time job. For the rest of the season, and in future years, regular tilling and hoeing should keep the weeds from overrunning the plot.

Dealing With Pests

Okay, let's talk about bugs. God put bugs on this earth for lots of different reasons. My husband says, "He put mosquitoes here so their larva could feed fish." But as far as I can tell, He put potato beetles here to eat potatoes and eggplant. (I guess God was a little pensive that day and decided that if gardening were too easy we wouldn't appreciate the goodies as much.) As for cabbage loopers, there is a certain magic in seeing how the ugliest critter ever to crawl can change into a beautiful white butterfly. The magic wears off, however, when you see how much damage it can do to your cabbages.

> **The good bugs will help manage the bad bugs.**

On the other hand, God also put praying mantises and spiders here to eat the bugs that are wrecking your harvest. Never forget about these beneficial insects.

I must honestly admit that I have occasionally used commercial pesticides, but I don't feel good about it. I'm not so much a pacifist that I will allow bugs to eat all my hard-grown veggies (although I have carried some pretty awesome bugs out of my house instead of stepping on them). I just feel that it's not smart to mess around with Mother Nature. Pesticides, besides being expensive, can mess up the balance in your garden. They kill good bugs as well as bad ones. So unless I have a rollicking infestation that threatens to ruin my garden, I leave the chemicals alone.

> **Chemical pesticides should be avoided.**

Fortunately, pesticides are not the only solutions. You can buy lady bugs and praying mantises and turn them loose in your garden. It's like keeping cats in the barn to eat mice—free cat food and free extermination. But bugs are flighty and cost a lot to buy.

A cheaper way is to grow the plants that insectivorous bugs like. Grow a patch of dill, or caraway, or fennel, and you can attract all sorts of good insects. You can also plant things that vegetarian insects don't like. For instance, aphids like almost anything that grows. But they don't like marigolds. So plant marigolds, and aphids will leave and look for another eatery.

Besides attracting beneficial insects, flowers in your vegetable garden perk up the place.

And even in a vegetable garden, a few marigolds can be extremely attractive. A little aesthetic beauty can provide a lot of pragmatic help to your gardening project.

For those interested in more direct action, there are some homemade remedies that kill pests safely. Three or four drops of liquid dish soap in water (rainwater or distilled water works best) makes a spray that will kill soft-bodied insects (such as aphids) when the water evaporates. The Safer company produces many environmentally sound insect remedies that are worth looking into. Ask at any good garden shop.

Finally, slugs go for beer in a big way. They're not fussy, so if a guest left a half bottle of beer last night, and it has gone flat, this is a good use for it. If you put a pie tin of stale beer in your garden with the rim at ground level, the slugs enter it and drown. I've heard that they drink themselves to death.

This Bud's for slugs.

You may also have problems with bigger pests. Woodchucks, for example, can destroy a whole season's worth of work in matter of hours. Raccoons have a taste for corn, and seem to know better than you do just when it's right for eating. And rabbits may be cute to look at, but they're a terror in a good garden.

77

There are all kinds of remedies to foil these greedy creatures, from wrapping corn in paper bags to spreading ground pepper and mothballs around the garden. Sometimes these remedies even work.

With critters, good fences really do make good neighbors.

You can set humane traps to catch animals without hurting them. All you have to do is drive the little cuties out to their natural habitats in the countryside and set them free.

Unfortunately, the only sure-fire solution to four-footed vegetarians is electric fencing. The same stuff that farmers use to keep cows *in* the pasture is just right for keeping critters *out* of your garden. The electricity isn't harmful, but once that pesky groundhog has touched it, he's not going to return to your garden, ever. Electric fence is expensive, but if you want to get the job done right the first time, it's the surest solution.

Handling Weeds

Weeds are another problem. One solution is to mulch. I mentioned black plastic earlier. This keeps the sun from shining on the little trespassers so only the vegetable plants peeking out through the holes you've made can grow. But you have to pay for plastic sheets. There are, fortunately, cheaper alternatives.

Mulching is a wonderfully lazy way to keep the weeds down.

When you mow the grass, save the clippings and use them as mulch around your plants. It's free, so why throw it away? (Let grass clippings dry out completely first, though. Fresh grass left in the sun can get astonishingly hot, and may burn tender seedlings.)

Leaves (preferably ground up with the lawn mower) also make an excellent free mulch. Other useful mulching materials include straw and shredded newspapers. (Use black and white only. Colored inks may contain toxic metals.)

Usually, weeding is a problem only if you let things get ahead of you, which, admittedly, can happen rather quickly in the summer. That's why you bought the hoe. If you drag it over your garden every few days, scuffling the surface, you will prevent the weeds from getting started in the first place. You will also avoid any chance of getting those bugs that sometimes like to sit out the heat of the day in mulch.

Weeding is easy, *if* you do it often.

Problem Soil

In the best of all possible worlds, plants get adequate nourishment from the soil. Most of us do not live in the best of all possible worlds. We live in places with poor-to-mediocre soil. To find your specific deficits, have your soil tested by the extension service, or do it yourself with a kit.

Soil comes in three types—clay, sand, and loam. Clay and sand have problems with draining. Clay won't, and sand won't stop. Good loam, unless you are lucky enough to inherit some, has to be built up. Clay soil needs sand and loam. Sandy soil needs loam. You can buy topsoil (that is, good, fertile loam) if you're in a hurry, but it will cost you dearly. If you're trying to save money, what you need is compost.

Where do you get compost? You make it. For free. Compost is simply decomposed vegetable matter. All vegetable matter will decompose, breaking down into rich nutrients that make the soil healthy and fertile. Properly made, and contrary to what you might expect, compost does not smell.

What rottin' luck!

You should have a compost bin. You can spend a lot of money buying a ready-made bin, or you can make your own. There are several ways. Wooden storage pallets standing upright will work—and you can usually get them free of charge. Hinge one of the pallets, so it can be opened like a door to remove the compost. Or you can use chicken-wire fencing, held up by stakes. Whatever you use, the bin should be about three by three feet, with plenty of holes to let in air.

Now that it's set up, start throwing in grass clippings, shredded leaves, weeds, and manure. Try to layer your work—six inches of vegetable matter, six inches of manure (if you can't get fresh manure, use high-nitrogen fertilizer), then three inches of soil. Water well, but do not soak. Throw in table scraps. (Never put in meat or bone, because these do not break down readily and can attract rodents, and *never* put in human waste. Serious diseases, including hepatitis and typhoid fever, can result from eating food fertilized with human waste.)

Even without testing your soil, adding compost will contribute to the best balance.

Turn your compost every week with a garden fork. The microbes in your pile need air to do their work, and unless you provide it, the pile can die. (You'll know it when this happens. The vegetable matter becomes heavy, wet, slimy, and a bit disgusting. It will also smell like. . . well, like something died.) Alive, it should get hot, around 150 degrees Fahrenheit. Within a few months, your pile will turn dark brown or black. When it reaches this point, it's ready. Now you can sift it, and work it into your soil.

Composting will also reduce your trash removal bill.

Is this beginning to seem complicated? It really isn't. And composting works, even if you don't follow all the steps with the recommended frequency. Any pile of vegetable matter will compost eventually, if it has adequate ventilation, even without watering, layering, or turning. It just takes longer, and the soil nutrients are less predictable. And even if composting hasn't completed by planting time, the organic matter will be useful if you work it into the soil.

No matter how poor your soil may have been to start with, a few seasons of composting will give you a rich and healthy garden that will provide plenty of cheap eating. It's the single best thing you can do for your garden.

A lazy way to compost is to bury your garbage in the garden.

Watering

In general, your plants need at least one inch of water per week. It is important to see that they get water on a regular basis, rather than simply to soak them when you notice that there hasn't been any rain for the last month. On the other hand, by mulching you can cut down the amount of extra water needed. Leave a large empty coffee can out in the middle of the garden and check it each week to see about how much rainfall you've had, then water accordingly.

Don't water in the heat of the day. You'll be wasting a lot of water to evaporation. Water in the morning when it's cool. Avoid the evening if you can, since plants that are wet overnight can encourage mildew.

The best time for watering is early morning.

Team Gardening

The old saying, "Friendships double our joy and divide our grief," is appropriate to gardening—especially if you have a large plot.

The trick to team gardening is division of labor. Unfortunately, some people are lousy gardeners. That's just the way it is.

Personally, I can grow vegetables in solid concrete, but flowers don't like me. I know this, and I would never go into a cooperative flower garden with someone else. Unfortunately, the only way to find out if gardening is for you is to get out there and do it.

If you have agreed to work with others in raising vegetables and you find out shortly into

Gardening season is a great time to develop your bartering skills.

81

the season that dirt is repulsive to you, bugs are unbearable, and the thought of getting on your knees in weeds is more than you can handle, you have to be fair. Confess up front and find a replacement pronto. Or talk with your partners and see if anything can be worked out. You might agree to do the canning, or show up at harvest time, fresh and ready to work when everyone else is exhausted.

Once you've made a commitment, try to stick with it, even if the going gets tough.

Do what you need to do to keep things upbeat. If push comes to shove, gird your loins, tell yourself that nobody ever died of gardening, and that you're saving a fortune. Then finish the season. Then, if you wish, vow never to do it again. But allow yourself a fair chance to change your mind. Come January, when you're opening a jar of tomatoes that you picked last August, or passing the ground hot peppers that you dried and crushed last September, or defrosting a bag of strawberries that you froze last June, you may decide it was worth it after all.

Superstitions

The word "superstition," like the word "cheap," gets a bad rap in America. I have developed a theory that virtually all superstitions have a basis in fact. In particular, don't be too quick to laugh off old gardening superstitions.

Superstitions are often truths that scientists haven't gotten around to proving yet.

For instance, Native Americans used to plant sweet corn in hills, three seeds to the hill—one to rot, one for the birds, and one to grow. Makes sense to me. Then there's the one about planting root crops in the "dark of the moon" and above-ground crops in the "light of the moon." The dark of the moon refers to the first and second phases, when the moon is waning from full to new (or dark). The third and fourth phases, when the moon "waxes fat" from new to full, constitute the light of the moon. I'm not sure if it really

82

works, or why, but what would it hurt to try? Farmers have planted this way for thousands of years, and it's kind of nice to follow this old saw, regardless of whether it's based on results or just tradition. After all, fantasy and fun won't cost you a dime!

Money-Saving Tips

Some crops save more money, with less effort, than others. One amateur gardener I know spent much of the summer tending to a potato patch. In the fall, he harvested about half a bushel, after throwing out the ones that underground pests had damaged. Since potatoes were in season, the farm markets were advertising them for about $4.80 per bushel. This gardener's efforts weren't totally wasted. He likes to eat the skins, and doesn't trust the skins of commercially grown potatoes that may have residues of fertilizers and pesticides. So he got a half bushel of potatoes with skins that he could trust. But in strict financial terms, he didn't get much per hour for his investment of labor.

Potatoes don't bring a large financial return because they are cheap to buy, especially when in season. And other than the issue of what may cling to the skins, garden potatoes are hard to distinguish from store-bought ones. Once they're mashed, the taste is pretty much the same.

Tomatoes, on the other hand, are easy to grow, and expensive at the store. And garden tomatoes taste better. Gardeners tend to think of tomatoes as a seasonal food. They eat huge quantities when they are harvested and plentiful. The greenhouse tomatoes, available in winter at the supermarket at high prices, are a pale, tasteless imitation.

Corn doesn't save much money in a small garden. It takes a lot of space to produce enough

Be sure to ask the old-timers for their gardening advice.

Begin with tomatoes and herbs.

for a few "corn on the cob" meals. And it depletes the soil, so you have to rotate it to another part of the garden, put extra effort into re-fertilization, or both. The meals may be worth the effort, but you didn't save much money per hour.

If you have a big garden, and plan to spend a lot of time at it, you'll want a variety of crops. But some will save more money than others.

If you have a small garden and limited time, concentrate on the money-savers—the things that are expensive to buy, easy to grow, and taste better than the pale imitations sold in stores.The list of money savers depends on your tastes. A good list to start with might include tomatoes, green peppers, broccoli, green beans, and lettuce.

Concentrate on easy-to-grow foods that are expensive to buy.

Asparagus is very expensive at the supermarket, and although it is a long-term project it doesn't require a lot of effort. If you like radishes, they're easy to grow, and take almost no space because they can be intermingled with other crops. If you're fond of raspberries or strawberries, starting a patch of your own may save big bucks in the long run. Perennials such as rhubarb, bunching onions, and horseradish will reappear every year with virtually no effort on your part, once they are established.

In short, if you don't have the time and space for a big garden, concentrate on the foods that your family likes, that are easy to grow, and that are expensive to buy in stores.

Check out nature's garden for wild edibles, too.

Gardening is a satisfying, healthful activity even if it doesn't save money. For many, the recreation and the enjoyment of home-grown meals are more important than the expense. But I find it more satisfying if, at the end of the year, I can document that it saved a substantial sum.

There are plenty of gardening books available. If you don't have one already, here are a few suggestions. Jerry Baker's *Fast Easy Vegetable Garden* (New American Library, 1985) is the simplest overall "how-to" book on gardening I have found. *Square Foot Gardening* by Mel Bartholomew (Rodale Press, 1981) shows how to get the most out of restricted space by planting in square-foot blocks rather than rows. It also has chapters on raised gardens and gardening to accommodate the wheelchair-bound. The "bible" for organic gardeners is Tanya Denckla's *Gardening at a Glance* (Wooden Angel, 1991). Another excellent resource is Dick Raymond's *Down-to-Earth Vegetable Gardening Know-How* (Garden Way Publishing, 1976). With gardening, there's no particular need to rush out and buy every new book that comes out. But new challenges will arise every year, and any serious gardener will want at least one or two trusted, dog-eared books to refer to.

Chapter 7
Can it! Keeping Your Harvest

Preserving food is the fine art of keeping it edible until you're ready to eat it. Methods include cold storage, canning, freezing, pickling, "jellying," drying, and smoking. These all can be done at home. A good book devoted to this topic is *Putting Food By* written by Janet Greene (Stephen Greene Publishers). In this chapter, we'll briefly check into what's best for you to use, what's cheapest, and why.

Cold Storage

With a cool, dry basement, you can preserve root crops such as potatoes, onions, garlic, turnips, and carrots for months. What could be easier? The ideal "root cellar" should be dark most of the time, should be fairly dry, and should be consistently cool. If you want to set aside a particular part of your basement for this purpose, check one of the many "build-it-yourself" books available at your local library. A root cellar can also double as a wine cellar, if you're so inclined.

Root crops are the easiest to save.

Freezing

Freezing is a terrific and easy way to preserve food. Take vegetables. Simply "blanch" your produce by slipping it into boiling water for one to three minutes and then immediately chill in cold water. This kills the enzymes that cause foods to deteriorate. Then pack your food tightly in freezer boxes or plastic freezer bags.

Freezing is the second easiest method of preservation.

Meat is even easier. Just wrap it in freezer paper or a freezer box. You can pack the meat in stock or not, but leave room for expansion because when foods freeze they swell.

Recycle food containers carefully.

> Don't freeze in glass jars unless the manufacturer says it's safe to do so. Glass that is not designed for freezing will break during expansion.

For energy efficiency, use a chest freezer, in a cool part of the house.

Freezer bags are initially cheaper than boxes but they can't be re-used. They also might not be good for thawing, and they're certainly harder to label. Freezer boxes (the plastic kind) cost more and they can be a pain to store, but you can let produce thaw in them and they can be re-used.

To make stacking easier for bagged foods, you can put the bags inside the boxes or other containers, such as milk cartons, until the food is frozen, then reuse the boxes. (If you open them carefully, you can save the cardboard boxes from commercially frozen foods for later use.)

When your freezer starts to look empty, add milk jugs filled with water. These will help hold the cold and lower electricity costs. They're especially handy in case of a power failure and also can be used in travel hampers.

There is a small appliance that heat-seals nylon bags. Once sealed, the bags (which come in many sizes) can be frozen, thawed, even boiled or microwaved to cook the contents! It saves washing dishes. It's convenient, but the bags are expensive and sometimes hard to find. You need to do a lot of freezing to make this worthwhile.

It's a good idea to be aware of what circuit your freezer is on, or what fuse its electricity passes through, in case something goes wrong.

One of my friends learned the hard way that her freezer in the garage was on the same electric circuit as her upstairs bathroom. Her family rarely used that bathroom, so there was no hurry to replace a blown fuse.

But while she complacently went about her daily business, strange forces were at work in her garage. Inside her freezer was a package of five loaves of unbaked bread dough. With no electricity, the bread dough—thawed.

A full freezer uses the least amount of electricity.

Do you know what happens to five loaves of thawed bread dough? They grow. They breathe and merge and mate. And they eat. In this case, they ate the large item bin at the bottom of the freezer, surrounding and consuming it. And still they grew.

Luckily, fate stepped in and saved my friend. She changed the fuse to restore the bathroom light. Just as the freezer door began to pulse, the fresh burst of cold, restored by the electricity, captured the drama. My friend was unaware of all this until she opened the door and found a horrible frozen monster—The Great Bread Blob.

Ice-filled milk cartons will help to protect food during a power failure.

It's still there. It has merged with the freezer. She fears that if she turns the freezer off, the blob will again find life. She checks her fuses often. It is an uneasy peace.

Canning

Canning, literally translated, means to store in cans. It's a little more complicated than that, though. The organisms that cause foods to spoil—bacteria, molds, and yeasts—float in the air. When foods go through the canning process, they must be heated enough to kill the bacteria, and the air in the can or jar is forced out, causing a partial vacuum. Since there is no air, no bacteria can survive, and the food remains sound. *Unless* the seal gets broken. If it does, air will

89

Canning is an art form. And if you do it well, your art will be admired.

enter and the food will spoil. That's why it's important to use jars that are in good condition (no nicks or chips). All your work will be for nothing if air seeps into the jar. That's also why the caps of two-piece lids can't be reused. Once they've been bent in opening, they won't reseal properly. Single caps can be reused with new rubber rings but frankly, I don't like them. It's harder to use jar rubbers and harder to tell if the seal is broken.

The expense of containers and equipment for canning is worthwhile only if the produce is cheap.

Never use old mayonnaise or jelly jars to can foods. Many weren't designed to withstand the pressure of the canning process and will break or even explode. Even if they do not, it is very difficult to establish and maintain an adequate seal. Only canning jars should be used for home canning.

Canning jars range from half-pint to half-gallon sizes. The initial expense of canning jars is not great, and if you know you'll be canning in the fall, it might be wise to buy a few jars each week over the summer. It's usually possible to buy canning jars and freezer containers at auctions, flea markets, or yard sales, for a very small cost. They may be chipped, so check before you buy. Other items you may have to buy are a colander, a ladle, a canner, and a jar funnel. You may want a food mill. Some friends or families go together to share the cost of a food mill (the Squeezo Strainer and Victoria Strainer are two excellent ones).

And, of course, you'll need a canner. You may want to consider a pressure canner. In my opinion, a pressure canner makes the whole procedure a lot more bearable. It lessens the time you have to spend processing your jars, and keeps the kitchen a lot cooler. A pressure canner also helps prevent botulism with the efficient distribution of heat under pressure.

Many people are afraid to use a pressure cooker because of the high-pressure steam. Today's pressure cookers have built-in safety releases that will blow to release the steam before the pot explodes. Unfortunately, depending upon what's in the cooker, you may have more than steam released. One relative, who wasn't watching her pressure gauge, strained cooked beans through the safety release. A modern art critic would have found the ensuing pattern of spray on the ceiling fascinating.

Watch your pressure gauge and follow your canner's instruction book to the letter. If your canner is old, talk with your extension office to see about having the gauge checked. You should also invest in a new gasket. Take care of these things well before canning season.

I would strongly recommend that you get a copy of the *Ball Blue Book* published by the Ball Corporation, Muncie, Indiana. This book is the home canner and freezer's bible, and tells you everything you need to know in clear terms.

So much for theory. Now for some unpleasant truths. Canning, unfortunately, is often a hot, messy, slow process. Let's consider a few examples.

A pressure cooker cuts time and cooking energy. And, no, you're not likely to blow yourself to smithereens.

Research the subject before canning for the first time.

Jellying

Reducing fruits to juice or pulp, and treating with sugar and a natural jelling substance called pectin, results in jelly, jam or preserve, mar-

You can make "jam" out of almost any mild-flavored vegetable—just add sugar, spices, and cook to the right consistency.

For health and good taste, try leaving the sugar out of the recipes for fruit butters. Gourmet restaurants have tried this with great success!

malade, and conserve. The difference is the amount of fruit and the thickness of the gel.

Jelly can be fun to make (surprise!), and really is not too much work. You can make several jars at once, and they're pretty as well as sweet. Canning companies make some lovely jelly jars that you might want to use for gifts. For everyday use, good old straight-sided half-pints are very nice.

Jam (or preserve) is jelly with pieces of fruit or pulp in it. Every so often freezer jelly or freezer jam becomes popular. The attraction, I guess, is that you needn't worry about it spoiling in the freezer. After you thaw it, it will keep for a couple of weeks in the refrigerator. Freezer jam and jelly don't have the same consistency as other jams and jellies, and many people don't like them. You may be one of the lucky ones.

Then there's marmalade. I doubt that many people are luke warm about marmalade—you either love it or hate it. I haven't made too much marmalade or conserve, but this isn't because it's difficult to make. It isn't. Conserve has a combination of fruits, usually with some nuts added. With more ingredients, it takes longer to prepare. It also costs more.

You don't have to limit yourself to fruits when you make jelly and preserves. Carrot jam is one of my favorites. You can also make green pepper jelly, tomato preserve, and what roast lamb would be complete without mint jelly?

Did I forget to mention butters? One of my favorite spreads is apple butter. Other gourmet delights include peach, pear, and tomato butter. Fruit butters are mashed pulp simmered with sugar (which is optional, and increasingly omitted by modern chefs) until the pulp is thick.

Pickling

There are two types of pickling—fermentation pickling and fresh-pack pickling. The vegetables usually used in pickles are cucumbers and green tomatoes, but you can also make good pickles with peppers, onions, cauliflower, watermelon rind, turnips, and peaches. Sauerkraut is fermentation-pickled cabbage.

Salt, vinegar, water (preferably soft), and spices are used for pickling. The spices are what make the difference between dill and sweet pickles, for example. Garlic also is often used.

In fermentation pickling, you prepare your "brine" or pickling solution according to the recipe you choose, and pour half into a pottery crock or other glazed pottery or glass container. (Do *not* make pickles in a metal container.) Add your cucumbers or whatever you've decided to pickle, and pour the remaining brine over the top. Put a plate on top, with a rock (clean, of course) for weight, if necessary.

The pickles need to be submerged under at least two inches of brine. The fermenting pickles will produce a foam or scum that should be removed every day. When the scum stops forming, the pickles are done. They should now be packed in clean canning jars and covered with brine. If the brine has turned cloudy, make a fresh batch, and process according to your recipe.

This procedure is kind of neat, and it gives you a feeling of real domesticity. But I have to tell you, it doesn't smell very good. It should have a tangy, yeasty odor, like beer. If the odor becomes especially unpleasant, sour, or very strong, check your pickles. If they are soft or slimy, something has definitely gone wrong. You may be a victim of "flat-sour."

Flat-sour is a type of food spoilage characterized by a soft food product with a slimy feel

Don't start making pickles if you're already in a sour mood.
—Country proverb

Fermentation pickling is an adventure in domesticity.

and an offensive odor. It attacks fermented products. If this happens, toss out the whole batch, then thoroughly clean and sterilize your crock and other equipment. If you don't totally destroy the molds, they may attack and spoil your next batch.

An easier method is fresh-pack pickling. Fresh-pack pickling is done by packing your food product in jars with the appropriate seasoning and letting it "pickle" right there. You can use either white or cider vinegar, but it needs about 5 percent acidity. Cider vinegar has a slightly milder taste. You should use pickling salt, but if you don't it won't hurt the product. The additives in table salt will just cloud the brine. Any minerals in the water can cause a reaction with the pickling spices. Remember that home-softened water has a lot of salt.

Fresh-pack pickling saves time and effort.

Drying

Drying is a dandy way to preserve because, with all the water out, food takes up much less room and requires no special storage equipment. You can spend lots of money buying cute little counter-top food dryers or floor standing dryers that handle lots of food. If your purpose in drying food is to pack a lot of food for hiking or camping, and you don't care if you spend some money for it, you'll have a great time picking your model. The rest of us, however, will probably use the sun or the oven. There's no difference in the finished product, no matter which method you use.

Sun-dried apple slices are a cheap snack food.

Home-grown popcorn is easy to dry. So are navy beans, pinto beans, split peas, and lentils. (Leave these on the vine until they have dried.) Raisins are dried grapes, and prunes are dried plums. Chili powder is dried chili peppers. Banana chips are dried bananas and are a wonderful snack, as are most dried fruits. They are very sweet because, as the water leaves, the sugar remains behind. Try dried fruit for your kids instead of candy. Growing and drying your own herbs (hang them upside down in an airy spot) can save you a lot compared to the price of the small, store-bought jars.

Dried fruit is a healthful substitute for candy.

Smoking and Salting

Smoking and salting have been used to preserve food for thousands of years. All you need for salting is salt—and sometimes water for brine preserving. Smoking requires something to smolder and an enclosed place for smoke to collect.

Dry salting requires packing in salt. The salt pulls the moisture away from the product. (Codfish is often salt dried. So is pork.) Salt-cured foods need to be thoroughly rinsed, and sometimes soaked, before cooking or eating. Brine curing is done by storing your product, such as ham, in a salt solution.

These techniques are uncommon in modern households, so I'll avoid the temptation to give detailed instructions here. If you're interested, find a book in the library. Or better yet, seek out a fellow enthusiast. People who preserve foods in this way tend to make a big project of it, and are eager to share their knowledge.

If you are interested in preserving foods, check with your library or extension office. Freezing and cold storage are fairly simple, but for other techniques, you will need to do your homework first. If you don't feel comfortable with a new procedure, consider taking a class at a local community college. Make sure your equipment is adequate and in proper working order. Date your preserved items so that you know how long you can expect them to last.

You might also find a canning cooperative in your area. For a modest fee or a portion of your produce, you will be able to can your harvest without investing in equipment of your own.

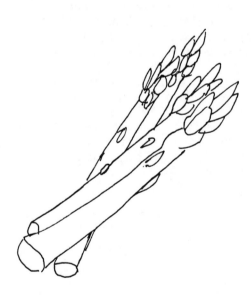

Chapter 8
Dieting and Other Eating Problems

There are dozens of special dietary needs that some people assume have to be expensive. I suppose if the doctor orders you to eat lobster Newburg, the devil with the cost. But you can still meet most nutritional needs on a tight budget.

Eating While Pregnant

In pregnancy, despite what your grandma said, you aren't really eating for two. Okay, technically you are, but if one of the two you're eating for weighs only three pounds, how much do you have to shovel down? Be sensible. You need to increase your *nutrition*, not your jowls. Your doctor or clinic will probably make suggestions on your diet, which you will, of course, try to follow, since you are responsible for the health and well-being of your baby.

Keep in mind that it's *not* a baby elephant.

Another problem in pregnancy is illness. It's cheap to eat when you can't face food, but it isn't good for you to skip eating if you're pregnant. Try eating several small meals instead of three larger ones. Avoid highly seasoned and greasy foods. Try soda crackers or dry toast and weak tea. Sometimes fruit helps. Finally, if nothing else works, remember that (thank goodness!) nobody has ever been pregnant forever.

In late pregnancy, constipation may be a problem. This can be alleviated by diet. Increase your fiber intake by eating more fruits and fruit juices, grains, and raw vegetables.

If you crave weird things, then normal foods are probably missing from your diet.

Many women have cravings during pregnancy, and if the yens are "normal" and don't interfere with good nutrition, there probably is no reason why they shouldn't be indulged. Cravings that are abnormal include laundry starch, chalk, and coal. Let me assure you, I didn't make these up. Pregnant women with nutritional deficiencies actually have craved these things, but these cravings should *not* be indulged, regardless of how cheap they are. Discuss these matters with your doctor.

Permanent Medically Restricted Diets

Don't fall into the "diabetic-dietetic foods" trap. Diabetic foods are generally sugar-free. Dietetic foods may have some sugar but generally less than other foods. (They also tend to have less fat and salt.) It's amazing how much companies charge you *not* to add sugar to their products. Fortunately, most of these products can be avoided without giving up good eating.

Refuse to pay more for something that was never added in the first place.

Instead of buying canned sugar-free fruits, buy whatever is in season; or buy fruits canned in light syrup, then rinse out the syrup. Instead of buying dietetic jellies and jams, buy fruit spreads sweetened only with fruit juice. Better yet, make your own. Remember that fruits have calories that enter quickly into your metabolism, but these can be accommodated in the "fruit exchanges" in your diet.

As far as sugar-free cookies and candies go, sure, you can buy them. But you also can suck on a frozen grape, which is just as sweet, takes longer to eat, and is a lot better for you. Also, if your diet allows dried fruit, you could have a little of that when you crave candy, as long as it's not coated with sugar.

Another permanent medical restriction is food allergy. This shouldn't weigh too heavily on the

98

food budget, unless it's for an extensively used food. An allergy to corn, for instance, rules out corn flakes, corn meal, corn bread, corn syrup, corn oil and corn oil margarine, corn starch, and popcorn. It also rules out anything made with any of these items as ingredients. A wheat allergy can make it seem as if everything were excluded: pasta, wheat cereals, crackers, pastries, and anything thickened with flour, such as cream soups, gravy and white sauce. (A spoonful of peanut butter will thicken gravy.)

To compensate for wheat allergies, you may substitute barley flour, corn flour, corn meal, rice flour, rye flour, oat flour, potato starch flour, or soybean flour. If the allergy is to gluten, however, you will need to eliminate, in addition to wheat flour, barley, rye, and oats. You may use arrowroot, cornstarch, corn flour and meal, rice, potatoes, tapioca, and soybean flours.

Few people have allergies to rice, and it's cheap.

Some of these things may be difficult to locate and will cost a bit more. Try looking at your grocery stores. If they don't have what you need, they may be able to order it. Check health food stores or food cooperatives that specialize in natural foods. The good news is that, although you may need to do more cooking from scratch, your end products should be cheaper than commercially prepared ones.

Co-ops are a good source of foods for special diets.

Allergies to eggs are easy to deal with if you cook at home. Because eggs are usually used in cooking as leavening or binder, try substitute agents. In baked goods, increase baking soda by half a teaspoon, and add binder ingredients. To bind fruit or sweet dishes, use two tablespoons of fruit purée (either mashed fruit or strained baby food). You also can use one teaspoon of unflavored gelatin mixed with two tablespoons of liquid. To bind vegetable or meat dishes, use two tablespoons of puréed vegetables.

The cheaper food may be better for you.

If you have an allergy to coloring and other additives—common in processed or prepared foods—you have a strong incentive to eat cheaply. You can prepare the counterparts to those foods, without the additives, at a fraction of the price.

Cholesterol

When you're on a cholesterol-restricted diet, it's easy to be taken in by all the advertising that claims to protect you from cholesterol. Perhaps aerosol cooking spray has no animal fat. But it's also many times more expensive than a very thin film of vegetable oil. Even better, try sautéing onions and celery in a couple of tablespoons of water.

No-name vegetable oil is as cholesterol-free as the expensive national brands.

Even if a recipe calls for frying, many foods can be steamed or baked instead. Vegetable oil and vegetable oil margarine, packaged generically or under a store's brand name, are as choles-terol-free as the national brands that make veiled promises to keep your heart and arteries from attacking you.

Use vegetable oil and vinegar with spices to make salad dressing, and bypass the special but expensive "safe" stuff in the grocery. If you're torn between two food items, the cheaper of the two often will be better for you. Chicken is usually less expensive than high-cholesterol red meat.

Feeding Kids

There are probably millions of different feeding problems connected with kids. Babies have whole books describing their peculiar nutri-tional needs. Then we have the finicky age, which continues to age 97 or so. Teenagers have not only the problem of non-stop eating but also the problem of a raging endocrine system that some doctors feel can be triggered or aggravated by diet. And finally, paying for all this frustration can be the biggest problem of all!

Breast feeding exclusively for baby's first six months is a lot cheaper than buying commercial baby food and formula. On top of that, mother's milk may have the best nutrition, and nursing may help you to regain your girlish figure. If you can do it, breast feeding is terrific. If you can't, or don't want to, that's perfectly all right, too. I firmly believe everybody should do whatever works best for them.

If you can manage it, breast feeding is cheap and nutritious.

The cheapest commercial formula is dry powder, if you're willing to do the work and supply the water. Don't give your baby iron-supplemented formula unless the doctor says to. It costs more and it might not be good for the baby. Some babies have a hard time tolerating the extra-iron formula, and vomiting can result.

Unless your cub scout has a craft project that needs the little jars (like the nail sorter every Dad must own), there is no reason to purchase commercially canned baby food. A lot of table food is already smooshed enough for an infant to handle—mashed potatoes, applesauce, ripe bananas. Other baby food is so easy and quick to make with a blender, or a food processor, or even a little plastic baby food grinder, that it seems a shame to spend lots of money on a jar of baby food that might have a shelf-life of five years. If you make baby food at home, you can spoon it into ice cube trays and put it into the freezer. When the cubes are frozen, just remove them from the tray and store them in plastic bags in the freezer.

Commercial baby food is a racket.

Once kids get out of the baby food stage, you're in real trouble. They learn that food is power. It doesn't take them long to learn where

Watch what you keep in the house. If you're eating junk food, the kids will want some, too.

Giving in to silly requests will probably lead to even sillier requests.

Try a "black and tan" sandwich if your kids are sugar-sensitive.

your buttons are. "Tammi's mommy lets her have ice cream before bed, not just milk like me. Is Tammi rich?" Or "I'm so upset that you won't let me have a dart gun, I can't eat. How long does it take to starve to death?" Or "I'll hold my breath until I turn purple."

How do you deal with a finicky eater? You *can* explain it, and should try to do so. But logic and reason don't always prevail. "Because I said so" has been an effective explanation for hundreds of years. It truly won't warp your child if you say no. (By the way, it might be a good idea to talk to Tammi's mom. Maybe she isn't really serving ice cream before bed. All the other parents in the neighborhood will be in your debt.)

Of course, your kids will probably experience treats and goodies and junk. But not exclusively, and not on demand, and certainly not because it is their due. Remember that if you do give in to silly requests, you will be doing neither your kids nor yourself a favor.

If your kids get "hyper" on sugar, try a black and tan sandwich—peanut butter with molasses, instead of jelly. It doesn't take much molasses to sweeten the sandwich, and you'll be adding iron and B vitamins, as well. (B vitamins are especially good for the nerves.)

Kids are very susceptible to suggestion. Ever know a kid who would go within a foot of cheese after somebody mentioned that it was made of sour milk? Think about sour milk. It's awful. It smells bad and tastes terrible. Isn't that enough to turn the stomach of any five year old? Heck, it turns my stomach.

I know of a young man who refused to eat hot dogs because somebody had told him they had earthworms in them. It said so right on the package. Sodium erythorbate. His grandmother

102

was able to get him to eat them by magic! She showed him a book that proved sodium erythorbate was a chemical made in a lab, and not something that had ever crawled. He was skeptical, but if grandma said it was so, it was so. He went to his friends and told them they were silly, and he was smart, and he had it in a book to prove it. All you need to do, sometimes, is listen to your kids. (The point here is not that you need encourage most kids to eat hot dogs, or anything with sodium erythorbate. But you can apply the same principle, straight talk and debunking of mythology, to healthful foods as well.)

When you allow kids to help fix the food, they have less resistance to trying something new.

Let us assume that you have listened, and that you have been understanding, and it still boils down to "I don't like it." Chances are that your child either doesn't know why, or can't put it into words. People often dislike foods because of the texture. Personally, I have trouble eating any seafood that contains grit. That eliminates roe, clams, oysters, and a whole lot of other things.

If junior dislikes one food, and it's not a major problem not to serve it, then wait a little while and quietly try it again without announcing what you're doing. The child's tastes may have matured by then. If, however, junior refuses to eat *any* type of fruit or vegetable, don't make the mistake of saying "You'll sit there until you eat every bite." You may wind up eating your words.

Angry confrontations over dinner are never constructive.

Try this. Start out with one half teaspoon of whatever it is that needs to be eaten. The child will eat it, just to make you look ridiculous. Then next time, serve the same amount. The third time, quietly increase it to one full teaspoon. It's still a tiny bit, and your child may not even notice the increase. The idea is to "vaccinate" the child. As your child gets used to it, gradually increase the portion. Take it very slowly. Kids remain kids for years. Even if it takes weeks—

103

Letting a teenager plan the meals and shop—with only so much to spend—may be a good learning experience.

and it might—it's still a painless way of teaching your child to eat all kinds of food.

This may not work. Some children can be stubborn. In which case, you might try treating your child as an adult. Give a simple choice for dinner: "Take it or leave it. This is what we are having for dinner. You don't have to eat it, but don't expect to get anything else." It brings home the message without discommoding you, and you won't have a battle of wills on your hands.

Of course, if you have a subversive nature, there is always the challenge of disguising the hated foods and sneaking them into the menu. Blender the unwanted veggies into a soup, for example.

There is a possibility that your child's food aversions could be related to an allergy. Be sure to check with your doctor if in doubt.

If small children pose problems by not eating enough, teenagers can pose the opposite problem. The open kitchen can get expensive. Do you have any idea how many steaks a teenage boy and his four or five closest friends can eat in an afternoon? I have, and it was enough to make me ill. Kids can cook a whole lot better than they can clean up, and full cabinets and freezers are a challenge to them. I decided it was time to make some rules. The law was, if you eat what isn't on the "okay-to-eat" list, you pay for it. My friend Bee decided to buy groceries a day at a time until her three teenagers got the point. This can be a very risky procedure, however. If she didn't plan carefully and follow her plan closely, she spent a whole lot more than she saved.

Foods planned for dinner must be off limits for snacking.

Losing Weight

Okay. Here it is—the magic formula for cheap weight loss. *Stop dieting.*

Yup. That's it. Look at the weight-loss section in your library. There are hundreds of different books. Now check the book stores—dozens more. Why do people keep buying every new title that comes out? Because the books don't work, that's why. One book doesn't work so they buy the next. If anything you're doing isn't working, just stop, step back, and take a long, calm look.

After losing an initial amount of weight by flushing out retained fluid, most people stop losing. The harder we try to count calories, the less success we seem to have.

Just say no to weight-loss diets.

Finally in desperation, some have been known to "splurge" on a three- or four-week supply of that stuff you mix with milk and use for two meals a day. Let me tell you, if you have never tried this, you don't know what you're missing. And you should keep it that way.

You and I know what's going to happen. We're going to cheat. Maybe sooner, maybe later, but it's going to happen. And after one little slip, we'll say, "The heck with it. I'll diet tomorrow." Or worse, "I'm a failure, what's the use?" Eventually then, whether we overcompensate or, as biophysicists believe, our bodies think we're starving so they add extra fat, the bottom line is, we end up *gaining* weight.

Dieting makes eating seem like a forbidden love affair.

You won't find a calorie chart in this book. I don't believe in them, except for special diets prescribed by physicians. A calorie is just a unit of energy, and not a saboteur.

I was once a calorie counter. I measured my meals to come out to no more than a thousand calories a day. After three weeks of this, I had lost only a pound and a half, about the same weight as three cups of water.

Dieting makes eating seem like a forbidden love affair

After my fiasco with calories, I decided that what I really had was a problem with carbohydrates. So I went on a carbohydrate-restricted diet. The results were eerie. I woke every morning at 6 a.m., bright-eyed and bushy-tailed. Any of my friends or family will tell you that when I'm ready to face the day before ten o'clock, something is definitely wrong!

I lost twelve pounds in a week and a half, and then wound up in a heap on the floor. I didn't take long to decide that there are worse things than being twelve pounds overweight.

Following that episode, I discovered the best, and the cheapest, way to lose weight.

Now I just *eat slowly*. It takes about 20 minutes for your brain to figure out that there's food in your stomach. That's enough time to gorge yourself and be miserable. If you eat slowly, and allow your brain time to catch up, you'll eat far less. Chew each small bite 20 or 30 times before you swallow, or count to ten after you swallow each bite before you pick up your fork again.

Chew each bite 20 or 30 times. . . or have a "slow race."

If there are several at the table who ought to shed a few pounds, you can have a "slow race"— to see who finishes last. Another trick is to go out of your way to make the meal a visual feast. When it's "too pretty to eat," your urge to "dig in" slows down.

A cooked-at-the-table dinner takes a long time to eat. Use a can of Sterno to heat a fondue pot full of onion soup. Serve a platter of bite-sized veggies and meat, chicken, or seafood. People can cook their own in the pot, and nibble on raw veggies while waiting. Fresh bread and a couple of fancy sauces can dress up this meal for company. It's easily expandable and a great way to cater to eating preferences.

Everybody likes cook-it-yourself fondue, and nobody gets fat from it. That's because it takes a while to cook it.

107

Fondue can be cheap, but it's easy to get carried away by the varieties. Here are a couple of money-saving tips. Look for a fondue set at tag sales—they're often cheap because so many people don't know how to use them. An alcohol burner—or for some types of fondue, a candle— may work as well as Sterno at a lower cost.

Regardless of what foods you serve, it helps to discard preconceived notions about eating. When you feel full, stop eating, even if there's food left on the plate. Don't eat just because it's lunch time or supper time—eat because you're hungry. If you had planned steak for dinner but decide that you really want only salad, then have salad.

Your brain will under- stand, soon enough, that you're just plain full.

Some of us were chastised as children about wasting food. As an adult, I figured out that forcing myself to eat food I neither wanted nor needed is just as wasteful as tossing food out the window. Mothers are at special risk—finishing up what the kids didn't finish.

Mothers are especially at risk.

Frankly, none of this works without regular exercise or, perhaps, changing a bit of your lifestyle. Hide the TV channel changer. Walk upstairs or down instead of taking an elevator. Then accept the fact that God did not intend all of us to have Madonna's figure. There is some great art to honor that.

Improving Nutrition

Protein doesn't have to mean steak every night. Dried beans, peas, and lentils are very inexpensive and an excellent source of protein. Another fine source is the humble soybean. It's very versatile—one of its many forms is "textured vegetable protein" or T.V.P., which can extend or substitute for meat.

Meat substitute can be found in vegetarian patties, links, and burgers. The patties and links usually come canned; the burger is dry and comes boxed. Soak it in hot water for 10 or 15 minutes to reconstitute it. Then mix with other ingredients for burgers or meat loaf. You can add this to spaghetti sauce or casseroles, too.

Even if you are not a vegetarian, plan several vegetarian meals each week, for health and savings.

Prices of meat substitutes vary, but they are almost always cheaper than meat and have little or no cholesterol. If they aren't available at your local grocery, your store might be able to order them. Soybean gravy mixes are available, to which you add only cold water. They're really quite good and have no fat.

It is possible to have a diet rich in high-quality protein while following a vegetarian-style menu. You must, however, use a variety of vegetable proteins to achieve complete nutrition. Frances Moore Lappe's 1971 book, *Diet for a Small Planet*, introduced the principle of protein complements. By combining a variety of foods, you get all the essential amino acids. One way to do this is by adding an equal proportion of protein from animal sources (meat, eggs, milk, etc.) to vegetable protein. Another strategy is to combine a food from the grain family (rice, barley, or wheat) with a food from the legume family (peas, beans, or peanuts). Nutritional experts now say that it doesn't matter when in the day you get the combination as long as the variety is in balance.

Make sure your family expects a variety of meals. That's the best way to cover nutrition and take advantage of the sales and the season.

Plan for adequate calcium. It might be as simple as drinking plenty of milk. Three tablespoons of dry milk has the calcium of one cup of whole milk, so mix dry milk into casseroles for added nutrition. Broccoli, kale, turnip greens, mustard greens, and collards are also high in calcium, a good source if someone in the family is lactose-intolerant.

If you don't like liver, many other foods are rich in iron.

You can increase your iron intake by eating red meat, especially liver or other organ meats. Liver is quick to prepare and inexpensive (unless, of course, nobody at your house will eat it). Egg yolks are high in iron, but cholesterol may be an issue, depending on which opinion you read. Dried beans, peas, and nuts are good sources. If beans are baked with molasses, the iron level is quite high. Dark green leafy vegetables are especially high in iron. (This means dark green *and* leafy. Green beans are *not* leafy, and lettuce is *not* dark green. Spinach, kale, and turnip greens fit the bill.) Dried prunes, peaches, apricots, and raisins are also high in iron.

Most libraries have an excellent collection of cookbooks, including those for special diets.

The cheapest sources of B vitamins are bread and cereal, dried beans, peas, and peanut butter. B vitamins are also found in meat, eggs, and green leafy vegetables. Citrus fruits, tomatoes, and green peppers have vitamin C. Potatoes also are reasonably high in vitamin C and low in cost. Rose hips are expensive unless you grow your own—rugosa roses will grow anywhere and bear plenty of hips. They'll make a good jelly, high in vitamin C. Vitamin D is found in milk and milk products, and fish oils, and you make your own when you're in sunshine!   Now that's cheap. When you watch your nutrition, you can eat cheap while you eat smart!

Chapter 9
Eating Out

First off, let's be honest. Eating out isn't cheap. Even a burger at a fast-food joint costs several times what you would have spent frying the same burger at home. If you are living on a tight budget, and can afford only what is essential, eating out is never absolutely essential. In this chapter, I'll assume that you have some mad money, and that you want the most bang for the buck.

If you've worked hard all week, eating out can be a delightful, well-earned indulgence. In my family, we think of it as a hobby. Not a cheap hobby, but no more expensive than, say, sky diving or raising llamas.

An "all you can eat" soup-and-salad bar may be one of the best eating-out bargains.

With that in mind, it's useful to think of your "eating out" budget as something separate from your regular food budget. But since it comes from the same source of income, you'll want to exercise common sense and self-control in spending it.

There are lots of places where you can eat for less than $15. For openers, you can go fast food. I have worked in fast food restaurants for years and still do occasionally. Lots of people look down their noses at fast food. Don't underrate it. If you get lots of greasy fried food and calories, it's your own fault and no one else's. Almost every fast food restaurant offers salad, and most have full dinners—not just sandwiches. I think fast food is one of the best buys for your restaurant dollar today.

If you are going out for dinner, why not try a restaurant with a salad bar? Or a chicken or fish place that has plate dinners? If you shop around, you can find a fast-food restaurant that offers a reasonably balanced meal for about $4 or $5 per person, plus beverage. That isn't bad for dinner out.

Pizza places vary greatly, both in price and in quality. (Of course it's much cheaper to make your own, but we're talking about eating out now.) Consider the kind of deal you're really getting, and avoid paying for "free" things you otherwise wouldn't buy. Some places offer a second pizza "free" for the price of one. Of course we all know it isn't free, but that's what they say. If the fourth topping is "free," but you want only three, you may be subsidizing somebody else's anchovies. Many places deliver, and if you eat in, you're helping to subsidize other people's "free" deliveries.

If the "free" things aren't what you want, then you're paying for somebody else's.

The bottom line is, *read* the menu. The prices at these places can be extremely arbitrary. Sometimes, if you order the "daily special" by name, it's half the price you'd spend if you customized the same pizza from the list of toppings.

A trip to our favorite national pizza chain store costs us under $15 for a large, thick-crust pizza with 11 toppings. That price includes soft drinks, and we take ample leftovers home for lunch the next day.

Whether or not a tip is expected might help you decide where to go.

Cafeteria-style restaurants are another option that saves on tipping. We have an excellent one where we live, and I sometimes go there for lunch. If you have school-age children, they may enjoy the opportunity to jump up during the meal to get napkins, straws, drink refills, toothpicks, etc. But if you have a baby or toddler, going through the line can be inconvenient. If you are carrying a diaper bag, pocketbook, and

112

shopping bag, too, a tray full of food could be just too much.

In that case, you might want to consider a family-style restaurant with high chairs or booster seats and table service.

Or choose a restaurant with an à la carte menu. If all you feel like eating is, say, a crepe and a salad, you won't have to pay for a lot of extras. Sometimes the "soup-and-salad-bar only" option is very reasonable, even at an otherwise expensive restaurant.

At a steak house, seafood may be expensive and inferior. The reverse may be true at a seafood restaurant.

Alcoholic beverages will crank up your tab in any place, but many of the small "mom and pop" restaurants that don't have a license to serve cocktails don't mind if you bring your own bottle of wine. State laws on this vary, so it may not be an option where you live. Call ahead and ask.

Churches and other organizations often have special suppers at a great price, an affordable night out while supporting a worthy cause.

Or you might want to get together with friends for a pot luck. Everyone brings one dish—salad or casserole or dessert or beverage or bread—to share. A variation on this is the "progressive dinner"—soup at one house, salad at the next, and so on. No one bears the entire expense of feeding a large group.

Since many of us like to eat out just for a change in routine, you might consider changing the routine without going out. Find a new recipe and serve it by candlelight in a room of your house where you don't usually eat.

Sometimes a picnic can be as much fun as eating out— because, after all, it is.

And if you're not doing so already, trade cooking nights with your mate for a rest from the kitchen.

Chapter 10
Back in the Kitchen

Avoiding Waste

Avoiding waste in all forms is the keystone of eating (and living) cheap. Here are some suggestions on how to do so.

If you are using your own, home-grown-without-pesticides vegetables, don't peel them. Instead, just scrub them vigorously. The highest concentration of nutrients in vegetables and fruits is often directly beneath the skin, and the peel is an excellence source of fiber. It is almost impossible to remove only the peel, which means that every time you take a peeler to a vegetable, you are stripping away the best part. The skins of commercial vegetables, however, may be a chemical screen you'd be better off to skip.

Another caution to consider is the green flesh directly under the skin of some potatoes. It is bitter and contains high concentrates of a chemical that can cause serious allergic reactions, and has been shown to be carcinogenic. Also, with potatoes, use only the tuber itself; cut away any sprouts, and *never* eat the leaves. What's wrong with the leaves? Well, the potato belongs to the genus *solanum*—a genus which also includes deadly nightshade. Need I say more? Incidentally, you should also never eat the leaves of rhubarb, another plant whose leaves are toxic.

If you do peel chemical-free vegetables, save the scraps. Many vegetable peels, such as carrot, turnip, parsnip, beet greens, and old spinach leaves or celery stalks make good soup stock. Just add water and boil. Onion skins will give a nice

Keep a jar marked "Soup" in the refrigerator for your scraps.

Yes, the skins *are* the best part, if they're not laced with toxic chemicals.

Are you pouring soup down the drain?

A rubber spatula can rescue another few spoonfuls of almost anything.

golden hue to the stock, but skim the tough layers out before serving. Don't forget to add any throwaways to your compost pile.

Never, but never, throw away the cooking stock from vegetables, poultry, or meats. Since the nutrients in vegetables that you boil cook out into the water, there's no reason to throw them away. Use them as a base for soup or stew. Stock from turkey, ham or beef is extremely valuable as a flavoring for soup, stew or casseroles. It's also useful as a base for gravy or flavored white sauce. Soup stocks can be frozen and are an indispensable part of good cooking.

You can get double duty out of beef, ham and poultry bones. Simmer the bones in water until every bit of meat comes off. If you add a tablespoon or so of vinegar, it will draw calcium from the bones and tenderize some of the tougher pieces. Then remove the bones, add vegetables, noodles, rice, barley, or potatoes, and you've got a good, nutritious soup. Ham bones can be used when cooking dried beans or peas, or with cabbage or green beans and potatoes. If you make a lot, you can freeze or can it for later.

Use the brine in pickle jars for seasoning potato and macaroni salads. The pickling spices add a nice tang to your dish.

Save margarine wrappers, and store them in a bag in the refrigerator or freezer. Use them to grease cake pans and to butter potatoes before baking. There is usually enough margarine left for those purposes, and your hands stay clean.

Don't throw away "empty" shortening cans. Save them for breakfast—you can usually scrape out more than enough residue of shortening to cook the family's eggs.

Store nearly empty cooking oil, catsup, and honey bottles upside down. Let gravity do the work. You'll get the last drop.

116

If you buy bread, save the wrappers. You pay for them anyway. Why throw them away and buy plastic bags? Just don't use them inside out with food exposed to the printing ink.

Usually, waxed paper is cheaper than plastic wrap, and wrap is cheaper than aluminum foil. Check out all your cereal boxes and snack bags if you've indulged. Most of the time you will find waxed paper and plastic linings that can be saved and reused. I also reuse aluminum foil and plastic wrap.

Bread bags have dozens of uses.

I save grocery bags. They're great for dozens of things, such as holding garbage, emptying the vacuum cleaner, or carrying lots of things when you have only two hands. I cut them open so they're flat, and drain deep-fried foods on them. I heard of a lady who lived in a dreary apartment and couldn't afford commercial wall paper, so she saved grocery bags and wallpapered with them. She stenciled decorations, and had a clean, lovely apartment at almost no cost. Bear in mind that some food warehouses will charge you for bags if you don't bring your own. That's another good reason to save them.

Some stores will take a few cents off your bill if you bring your own grocery bags.

Some kids love to draw, color, finger paint, or block print (using food coloring and a "sculpted" potato) on grocery bags that have been cut open. Their creations can make colorful wrapping paper for grandparents' gifts. To make the paper somewhat glossy and waterproof (after the artist has finished,) place waxed paper over the top and press with a warm iron.

Cover and refrigerate leftovers at once. Most cooked foods begin to deteriorate within two hours if left standing at room temperature. At that point, you start risking spoilage and food poisoning. It may look fine, and the more reckless members of your family may want to sneak a bite, but this is not something you should go along with. (Not that it will happen more than once anyway. Believe me, if you have lived through food poisoning once, you will never risk it again.) A good rule of thumb is, if cooked food stays unrefrigerated overnight, throw it out.

Don't freeze packaged meat in the grocery store wrap, by which I mean the kind that has a little foam or paper tray on the bottom and plastic wrap on top. Air passes through this kind of packaging, and your products will get "freezer burn" very quickly. The dried out products are unappealing, poor-tasting, and very non-nutritious. There is no cure, and—you guessed it—you have to throw your meat away. (Okay, you don't really *have* to. Meat burned by the cold probably isn't going to hurt you, but it certainly won't taste very good.) To avoid freezer burn, use freezer paper, freezer bags, or boxes. If you have old bread bags, this is an excellent use for them.

It's a good idea to label your leftovers in the refrigerator, and it wouldn't hurt to date them as well. Do the same with everything in your freezer. Frozen food doesn't last forever, no matter how well sealed. You should have an idea of what you have, so you can use it before it spoils. You can buy bags with cute little labels included, but you pay a lot for those labels. Paper is cheap. So is tape.

Freezing flour and corn meal will prevent weevils or mealy bugs. Just put the entire package into a plastic bag and seal it.

Empty cardboard milk cartons can be opened up and used to keep table scraps until you're ready to throw them out or (better yet) onto the compost pile. By the way, you can put this waste in the freezer if you're concerned about odor. The bacteria that cause odor will become dormant and won't stink up the kitchen.

One way to get rid of leftovers is to leave them in the freezer until they are no longer edible. Clean out your freezer *at least* every three months.

Clean empty milk jugs or cartons can be filled with water and frozen. Then you have free ice for your ice chest for picnics. Also, if your electricity goes off, you can put these on the top shelf of your refrigerator to help keep your food cold.

If you're into crafts, milk cartons make great candle molds. They also make nice fireplace logs—if they're coated with wax rather than plastic. Open the top completely, roll newspapers tightly, and pack them into the carton. Throw the whole thing on the fire. The wax will catch fire easily. The tighter the newspapers are rolled, the longer they will burn. It's a lot cheaper than paper-wrapped, store-bought fireplace logs.

This brings us to newspapers. I never throw them out. You can use newspapers instead of cloth or paper towels for cleaning windows. They don't leave lint, and newsprint makes windows really shine. Newspaper is also good for soaking up oily spills, and other major messes, such as dog vomit, prior to final cleanup.

Newspapers aren't just for training puppies.

Don't line bird cages with colored newspapers. Unlike black and white, colored newspapers may contain lead that can kill your birds.

One friend uses comics and brightly colored flyers for wrapping paper, tied with a bit of yarn. When kids demolish the wrapping in two seconds flat, there are no regrets.

Wrapping paper for free!

If you can't think of enough to do with your newspapers, take them to a recycling center, or donate them to the local newspaper drive. Do not, however, allow them to sit for months in a corner of the garage. With no help from anyone, they may spontaneously combust and burn down the building. (Some people think this happens only with oily rags. Not so. It also occurs with paper, damp hay, and a lot of other materials.)

Products with lots of packaging always cost more, and the extra wrapping is a burden to our landfills. A good example is "variety packs" of cereal. What's the point of paying somebody to measure out a piddley little bowl of cereal for you? The last time I checked, corn flakes were 11¢ an ounce in regular boxes, but 31¢ an ounce in cute little boxes.

What's the point of paying someone else to measure out a piddley amount of cereal for you?

The same applies to drink packs and chips. You can buy a 14½-ounce bag of chips for $2.79 and portion the chips into 14 or so reusable sandwich bags instead of buying nine one-ounce mini-bags for the same price. Avoiding waste can take will power, however, if there's a chance that someone will devour the whole thing once the bag of chips has been opened.

Keep your garbage to a minimum—in most parts of the country, the cost of getting rid of it is increasing rapidly. And plastic bags, which most trash removal companies now require, are also expensive. Crush tin cans, flatten cereal boxes, and do anything else you can think of to reduce the bulk.

Make a can squasher with two 2-foot pieces of 2-by-4, hinged.

Better yet, save even more money by recycling. In a sense, you're already doing this by reusing your newspapers and putting vegetable wastes on the compost pile. Find out where the local recycling center is in your community. Generally, the folks there will be happy to take glass, newspaper, cardboard, tin cans, plastic milk jugs, and often other material. Best of all, unlike the garbage companies, they probably won't charge you for hauling the stuff away.

If you're a renter and the landlord takes care of the trash, maybe you could offer to supervise recycling in the building and split the saving. One family of four went from five bags of garbage every week to just one every other week, as soon as everyone was careful to recycle.

On the bright side, some packaging can be a bonus. Jelly jars can become free drinking glasses. Mayonnaise jars provide perfect see-through storage for rice, beans, or barley, and the glass will be a great frustration to any errant mouse roaming about. I also keep wooden matches in glass jars, especially when we are camping, to keep them dry. Restaurant-size pickle jars are a perfect size for a canister set.

Old jars needn't be unattractive. You can paint the lids to suit your kitchen decor.

Of course, you'll save a lot more money by making your own baby food, but glass baby food jars are terrific for spices. Fasten the lids to the underside of a wall cabinet with mastic or small screws and make an attractive label for each. Then you'll be able to unscrew the jar with one hand while cooking. The little jars are also useful in the work shop to organize odd pieces of hardware (screws, nails, hinges, faucet washers, and all those other things that you can't quite bring yourself to throw away). Or to sort buttons and snaps in a sewing basket.

If you don't have a baby (or make your own baby food) perhaps you can barter to get some of these jars without having to buy them.

How do you get baby food jars if you don't have a baby? Offer to barter, even if you have to introduce yourself at the check-out counter.

Equipment and Supplies

There are a great many pieces of equipment that you can cook without. Some are downright silly—things like electric potato peelers and revolving spice racks. You'll notice a lot of them advertised right before Christmas, and never again (which gives you an idea as to how useful they really are).

There are, however, some items that I rely on in the kitchen:

Pots and pans serve the same function as "cookware," for a fraction of the price.

Rubber spatula
Folding steamer basket
Metal spatula
Mixing bowls (2 to 4)
Wooden spoon
Measuring spoons
Vegetable peeler
Measuring cups
Paring knife
Wire whisk
Large butcher's knife
10-inch skillet with lid
Muffin pan
9-inch cake pan
2 loaf pans
1- and 2-quart pots
2 cookie sheets
2-quart covered casserole
2 can openers (one crank, one "church key")

Trail cooks use a deep cast-iron pot called a Dutch oven for everything from scrambled eggs to birthday cake.

This list is neither extensive nor expensive, but each item will simplify your life and encourage you to cook.

Small Appliances

There are no small appliances that you *must* have to cook cheaply and well. However, to make cooking quicker and easier, *some* electric appliances are a terrific help. As a general rule, limit yourself to the appliances that can be put to a lot of different uses. A food processor, for example, will do everything a blender will do except liquify. And it's a lot easier to use. Get only what you know you will use. If you have any doubt as to what is merely clutter, check out a few local garage sales and see what outlandish appliances your neighbors are trying to get rid of. They may have learned the hard way what appliances end up being superfluous. On the other hand, you may also find second-hand bargains on genuinely useful items.

Millions of slicer-dicers are sold each Christmas, then sold again at summertime garage sales.

Here's a list of electric appliances that may be useful:

Toaster oven
Food processor
Electric beater
Microwave oven
Electric frying pan
Automatic coffee maker
Popcorn popper

When you use any small cooking appliance, you'll be using less electricity than an electric stove consumes for the same task. But if you have to run several at once, the oven might be cheaper. And don't use energy saving as an excuse to go out and get a new gizmo right away. If you have to buy an electric frying pan new, for example, it could be five years before you save enough electricity to recoup your $30. Look for bargains at a yard sale or put useful items on your birthday wish-list.

An apartment-sized oven uses less energy than a full-sized one.

There are, by the way, a few expensive gadgets that are genuinely fun to use. Examples include bread-making machines, juicers, and fruit dryers. Your family may get more enjoyment from these things than from, say, the latest video game machine. And they provide an incentive to eat nutritious foods. The kids may argue over who gets to make the next loaf of whole-grain bread, or they may give up soda pop in favor of carrot juice. But none of these gadgets is essential to a well-equipped kitchen. And there are far cheaper ways to make nutritious foods taste good.

123

Energy Savers

Cutting down the size of items to be cooked can shorten the cooking time considerably. If you are making mashed potatoes, cut the potatoes into small pieces first. If you're baking them, cut them in half and put them face down on a cookie sheet. Stainless steel or aluminum nails thrust through a potato will speed cooking, but be careful about using just any old nail—some are coated with chemicals.

One great trick from the book *Cheap Tricks* by Andy Dappen is to cut a quarter-sized hole in hamburgers to speed cooking. You can make hamburgers the same size you normally do, but they'll cook faster, with less energy, because they will have more surface area.

Holey hamburgers!

If you are using the oven to fix a meal, figure out how much you can get into it. For example, instead of cooking green beans on top of the stove, put them in a covered oven dish to heat, next to the meat loaf and baked potatoes. If you'd rather have mashed potatoes, put that pan (with potatoes and water) in the oven, too. It will take a little longer than the top-of-the-stove method but not much if the pieces are small.

The more food in the oven, the more efficient it is.

Turn off the burners before everything is ready. Scrambled eggs will continue to cook in the heat of the pan. And sliced carrots will finish cooking just fine in five more minutes of hot water. This is especially true with an electric stove, since the burners stay hot for a while after they are turned off.

Cook in batches and freeze what you don't need right away. That way you'll have a ready casserole or pie that, once thawed, may need only a quick zap in the microwave.

Chapter 11
Something from Nothing

I am baffled by people who tell me they never use leftovers. They look upon them as garbage, or, at best, something to feed to the pets. I look on leftovers as spare change. After all, when I use a dollar bill to buy something that costs 75¢, I don't tell the cashier to keep the quarter. Not using leftovers is throwing away money.

There are lots of things you can do with leftovers to make them appear fresh, appetizing, and, yes, even "new."

Here are some suggestions—general and specific ideas—listed in no particular order. Just browse through, and make a mental note of any ideas you'd like to try. Since every assortment of leftovers is different, using them is a creative process, heavily influenced by your own styles and tastes. Once you get the hang of it, you'll be inspired to come up with your own unique ways to turn leftovers into tasty, nutritious, and even elegant meals.

- If you misjudged the appetite of your breakfast crew and end up with lots of pancake batter, go ahead and cook the full batch. Then use the leftover pancakes as "crepes" for lunch or dinner. Choose a filling, such as meat-and-mushroom gravy or any green vegetable with ham and cheese. Roll a pancake with the filling, secure it with a toothpick, zap in a microwave, and top the whole thing off with mayonnaise or horseradish sauce. If you freeze pancakes, you can heat them up in the toaster for a quick breakfast.

When I use $1 to buy something that costs 75¢, I don't tell the cashier to keep the quarter.

Anything left over can enhance a later meal.

125

• Bacon ends and pieces, if used in small quantities, can add a lot of flavor to a main dish without adding too much cholesterol. A small amount of chopped bacon cooked with pinto beans and served with corn bread—or cooked with rice and added to soup—can add a lot of interest to an otherwise meatless meal.

If you wait two weeks to clean out your refrigerator, you'll be making compost— not soup or a casserole.

• Leftover smoked or Polish sausage can be sliced and cooked with eggs or spread over a pizza. Likewise, hot dogs can be chopped and mixed with beans, tomato sauce, brown sugar, and onion for a beans-and-franks casserole. It's amazing how the same two hot dogs that won't feed two hungry kids will suddenly feed a family of four and seem like a lot.

• There are countless ways to combine small amounts of several different types of meat—in hash, meat loaf, or shepherd's pie.

• Leftover cooked and raw vegetables can be combined to add interest, and nutrition, to a tuna-macaroni salad or even a tossed salad.

If you need a good broth to start a soup, ask the meat clerk for a "dog bone" —even if you don't have a dog.

• Soup is a great way to clean out a variety of leftovers from your refrigerator. A couple of carrots, one large potato, an onion, a cup of green beans, some rice and pasta will go together nicely. Add a little corn, and perhaps a tomato or two if you have them. If you can round up a soup bone, a leftover turkey leg or chicken wing, or even a bouillon cube, so much the better.

• Try frying leftovers with garlic and other spices. If the motley collection in your pot screams "leftovers," it's a good time to experiment. One trick is to purée the mixture in a food processor and give it an exotic name, such as "Russian Winter." Top it with a little embellishment—three curls of shredded cheese, some croutons, or a sprinkle of red pepper. This

127

Dumplings are cheaper than rice or potatoes.

You don't have to feed dry bread to the squirrels— make your own stove-top stuffing.

should impress your guests! Or freeze the concoction and let it reappear on the menu when it will be a "new" dish.

• Stew is just thick soup with bigger chunks in it, so if you have chicken, turkey, leftover roast, or even hamburger, you can make a stew. (On the other hand, if you have leftover stew you could thin it with broth and call it soup.)

• Dumplings can make any soup or stew into a new meal, regardless of how many people show up for dinner unannounced! Season the dumplings with herbs or some of your dried-up old cheese, grated, for a bit of flair.

• Casseroles are another creative way to combine leftover vegetables, meats, pasta, rice, potatoes, etc. into a delicious new meal. Just add whatever is short in the balance (macaroni or rice, for example, or if there's no leftover meat, perhaps a can of tuna). Then mix in some white sauce, season to taste, and bake.

• What if you have one serving left of stew, hash, or casserole, and you don't feel like recycling the ingredients again? It might make a great change-of-pace breakfast or lunch for one person. Just zap it in the microwave.

• Freeze odd bits of cheese. Rinds of parmesan or romano are essential to a good minestrone. Old cheddar can be used in rarebits or soufflés. Shredded or cubed, cheese can top tacos or fill up omelettes. Cottage cheese, even if it's been frozen, can be baked into lasagna.

• Keep a bag in the freezer just for crusts and other stale (but not moldy) breads. Then use for croutons, stuffing, bread crumbs, meat loaf, or to extend a variety of dishes.

128

• A "stir fry" meal is one way to throw lots of little bits together and make it look planned that way. Shred and fry any random fresh veggies that you have on hand, then add the already-cooked leftovers at the last minute, and doctor the whole thing with soy sauce and ginger.

• If you have one pork chop, or half a cup of hamburger or a tiny bit of leftover steak or chicken, cut it into small cubes, and sauté with some onion and celery tops, plus any other seasonings that might spark up the taste. Add two cups of raw rice, and four cups of liquid (water, bouillon, or tomato juice), cover, and simmer for 15 minutes, then pop into a 350-degree oven for 30 minutes.

To make sure you have enough left over for another meal, *you* do the serving or hide away the part you want to save.

• Leftover pot roast has hundreds of uses, but here's one you may not have thought of. Chop it in a blender with onion and mayonnaise for a nutritious, tasty sandwich spread. (If you have one, a stalk of celery makes a dandy spatula to push the mixture into the blades.)

• Add any leftover meat to gravy or white sauce and serve over noodles, rice, toast, mashed potatoes, or home-made stuffing. A little meat can go a long way.

Rinse the jelly jar with hot water.

• To leftover mashed potatoes, just add milk, eggs, and flour to create potato pancakes, which are good at any meal.

• Leftover jelly can be melted with a little hot water and used as pancake syrup.

• The last dredges of fruit gelatin can be flaked by running fork tines through it. Spoon this into a parfait glass with alternating layers of whipped topping to create a one-person snack. Leftover pudding can be layered in a parfait glass with some leftover cake or cookie crumbs, fruit, or whipped topping.

129

Stretch a fruit cobbler with bread crusts and cinnamon.

• Leftover fruits are perfect for a fruit salad, or for pie filling. If your fresh apples are beginning to be less than crisp, there's nothing wrong with slicing them into a pie. The same goes for aging cherries, peaches, and berries, and, heck, throw in the grapes from the bottom of the fruit bowl, too. Perhaps you don't have quite enough for a full-sized pie. In that case, you could make a cobbler. And if you still need to stretch that, get some of the frozen chunks of stale bread (crouton-size) out of the freezer and mix them in—with lots of cinnamon, of course.

• Bananas that are beginning to turn black are the perfect sweetness for banana-nut bread, muffins, or pancakes.

You get the idea. There aren't many things that you have to throw out if you just use your imagination. Some people think that dealing with leftovers takes a lot of time or effort, but how much strain is it to tear or cut up pieces of bread and throw them in the freezer, or to put a little water in the last of the jelly? In truth, cooking with leftovers is often faster and easier than cooking from scratch. After all, part of the preparation has already been completed!

Chapter 12
Recipes for Cheap Eating

Government surveys in 1989 said that the minimum, rock-bottom grocery budget for a U.S. family of four was about $75 per week. But when I examined the list that the USDA used for their "Thrifty Food Plan" I found some things that were not particularly healthful and others that definitely were not thrifty, with an abundance of expensive red meats. Although I sometimes might buy these items if they are on sale or if I have an irresistible urge to splurge, a thrifty shopper would not buy:

> sour cream
> canned chili
> canned stew
> ready-made soup
> ham
> steak
> soft drinks
> fruit "punch"
> pancake syrup
> store cookies
> boxed cereal

This list includes the problem I mentioned with expensive breakfast habits. Boxed cereal costs far more than most other choices. Pancake syrup isn't a great choice either, having little nutritional value. For example, applesauce makes an excellent topping for pancakes, waffles, or french toast. It is not only nutritionally better than syrup, it allows me to avoid using a high-sugar product that would make my kids "hyper." Cheese sauce is another alternative. Or by adding vanilla and cinnamon to the batter, a piece of french toast will be quite tasty as is, with only a dab of margarine perhaps.

Here is a sample shopping list to feed a family of four for $30 or so (based on prices in Ohio, late 1992). It takes advantage of low-cost, high-nutrition foods. Vinegar and oil and salt and pepper are missing from this list, but in another week—with baking powder, potatoes, and flour left over—you can add more staples and still stay close to $30. If you find it hard to schedule time to make bread by hand, substitute bread from a bakery thrift store. The price will be about the same, but the bread won't be as delicious.

$1.26	3 lbs. onions
.89	2 lbs. carrots
1.06	10 lbs. potatoes
1.59	3 lbs. apples
1.47	3 lbs. bananas
1.98	2 lbs. grapes or a melon
.50	1 small head cabbage
.89	1 bunch escarole or lettuce
.69	spinach
.39	1 bulb fresh garlic
1.29	frozen orange juice (12 oz.)
1.39	peanut butter (18 oz.)
.85	baking powder (10 oz.)
.95	5 lbs. flour
.75	1 lb. brown sugar
.79	1 lb. box macaroni
1.05	yeast, 3-pack
.45	1 lb. popcorn kernels
.38	1 lb. lentils
.69	1 lb. rice
.79	1 can tomatoes (28 oz.)
.33	1 can corn (15 oz.)
.33	1 can kidney beans (15 oz.)
1.18	2 doz. eggs
.30	1 lb. margarine
3.78	2 gals. milk (or large box powdered milk—8 qt.)
1.18	1 lb. ground turkey or a good buy on chicken
.99	1 lb. hot dogs
2.20	4 cans tuna (6½ oz.)
$30.39	

The following menu shows one way to get through the week on this kind of budget. Home-made herb tea is a nice addition if you didn't include coffee in your shopping list.

Breakfast	Lunch	Dinner
Milk or water	Milk or water	Milk or water
Potato pancakes	Egg salad sandwich	Creamed turkey with dumplings
Applesauce	with lettuce	Cooked carrots
	Grapes	Banana bread
Milk and juice	Milk or water	Milk or water
Muffins	Peanut butter sandwich	Lentil and rice casserole
	Applesauce	Sweet and sour cabbage
	Carrot sticks	Garlic bread
Milk or water	Milk or water	Milk or water
Pancakes	Tuna sandwich	Scalloped potato casserole/hot dogs
Banana	Grapes	Baked onions
		Carrot-apple salad
Milk or water	Milk or water	Milk or water
French toast	Coleslaw with apples	Mexicali casserole
Grapes	Bread and butter	Salad
	Peanut butter cookies	Baked apples
Milk or water	Milk or water	Milk or water
Muffins	Salad	Tuna macaroni casserole
Banana	Garlic bread	Spinach
	Grapes	Carrot sticks
Milk or water	Milk or water	Milk or water
Waffles	Peanut butter sandwich	Omelette
Applesauce	Carrot sticks	Hash-brown potatoes
	Banana	Salad
		Biscuits
Milk and juice	Milk or water	Milk or water
Muffins	Egg salad sandwich	Leftovers soup
	Apple	Garlic bread
	Peanut butter cookies	Coleslaw

Snacks: popcorn, fruit, banana bread, cookies

I certainly wouldn't expect your family to follow this shopping list and this menu plan week after week. It's just an example of what you can do with careful planning. For another week, I might buy a chuck roast instead of the turkey and hotdogs and plan at least two meals from the roast. If you grow a garden, can and freeze foods when they're in season, buy in bulk, and cook creatively, you should be able to craft a more elegant menu plan at an even lower average cost.

But if you're a typical family, you'll occasionally give in to steak fits and potato-chip orgies. You're likely to want some empty-calorie desserts, along with gourmet treats that have expensive ingredients. That happens in our household, too. But because it's possible to eat fairly well for $30, I have a lot of leeway for indulgences while still spending far below the average.

The recipes in this chapter are examples of how you can eat well, without spending a fortune, although the recipe for lasagna shows how pricey a "standard" menu item can be. Some of the recipes are new, but many are old stand-bys. I've included them— along with the cost for each—because, until I actually figured the dollars and cents, I was only guessing about cheap food. I think you'll find it enlightening. Yeast, for example, is nearly half the expense of making bread. With that news, you might want to develop your skills with sourdough cooking.

By the time this book gets to print, the prices may be dated. Furthermore, there are bound to be extreme differences from one part of the country to another. (As an isolated example, my editor in Vermont says that egg prices are higher there than what I have listed.) But these prices—gathered in Ohio in late 1992—should at least give you a ratio of expenses as a guide. Or perhaps they will motivate you to do your own price comparisons for the meals you usually plan.

In costing-out recipes I have not included the price of most leftovers, since that cost would be calculated in the initial recipe. I also have not included any optional items, shown in parentheses in the ingredients list. The variations in cooking and quality of ingredients are many, so all costs are approximate. Even though I buy some things most often at the discount store, I took an average of prices available from three local stores. If an item cost less than a penny, I have counted it as 1¢.

Many of the recipes are given using dry milk but will work just as well using fresh milk in place of the water (increase the amount of milk a bit). The exact quantities are not critical for most recipes.

Casseroles and Main Dishes

Any casserole can be created using starch (noodles, rice, and potatoes, etc.), protein (meat, eggs, cheese, etc.), vegetables, and sauce. Garnish as desired. This is why leftovers are so great. You can make a casserole and everybody thinks you planned the whole thing from scratch. Be adventurous!

I have included some meatless casseroles. These have a combination of grains and legumes—or sometimes a dairy product—and provide sufficient protein as is—no meat needed. These are high in fiber and low in cost!

Don't forget that soups and stews can be "main dishes," too.

White Sauce
Sometimes called "Milk Gravy"

I	II
(equals 1 can cream soup)	(full recipe)
¼ cup dry milk	½ cup dry milk
2 Tblsp. flour	¼ cup flour
dash salt	½ tsp. salt
1 cup cold water	1¾ cup cold water
1 Tblsp. margarine	2 Tblsp. margarine

Melt margarine in a 1-quart sauce pan. In a covered jar or shaker combine dry ingredients and mix well. Add water. Shake until all ingredients are dissolved. Stir in flour-milk mixture and cook over low heat until mixture thickens and bubbles. Keep stirring.

Cost of Cream of Mushroom Soup: 58¢   **Cost White Sauce I: 7¢**

Variation: **Chicken Sauce**—Substitute cold chicken stock or cooled prepared chicken bouillon cubes to the sauce as it thickens. Omit the salt.   **Cost: 12¢**

Cheese Sauce I—add ½ cup of processed cheese cubes or shredded natural cheese to version I. Heat over low heat, stirring constantly until all cheese is melted.   **Cost: 44¢**

135

Cheese Sauce II (microwave method)—In a ceramic gravy boat combine 1 cup water, 6 Tblsp. dry milk, 2 Tblsp. flour, dash of nutmeg, and hot sauce. Stir in flour and add ½ cup of cubed cheese. Zap, watching carefully. As it starts to boil, stop and stir. Continue until all cheese is melted. **Cost: 64¢**

Creamed Chipped Beef—Shred chipped beef (2½ oz.) and sauté in the margarine for about 1 minute. Add flour and water mixture to dried beef, stirring constantly until mixture bubbles and thickens. Serve on toast, pancakes, potatoes, or noodles.

Cost with potatoes: about $1.46

White Sauce III

2 Tblsp. margarine
¼ cup flour
1¾ cups cold water
½ cup dry milk
salt and pepper

Here is an alternative way to make a cream sauce. Melt margarine in a frying pan. Add flour and work into a paste or roux. Mix powdered milk and water and add quickly to the roux, stirring rapidly to avoid clumping. **Cost: 7¢**

For **Creamed Peas on Toast**—Once the cream sauce has thickened, add 1 can peas and 4 hard-boiled eggs, chopped. (Note: this was originally a depression-era treat, good enough to evoke nostalgic memories among people who insist that it's not genuine unless you use canned peas. Modern gourmets, discovering it for the first time, may possibly prefer frozen or fresh peas.) Serve on toast, potatoes, or noodles. **Cost counting 8 pieces of toast: $1.12**

Variation: for **Tuna-Pea Wiggle**, add a can of drained tuna. (You could skip the eggs, if you prefer.) You can be as creative as you want with this recipe—mixed veggies and onions also taste good. **Cost: $1.63**

Gravy

Whether it's pot roast, pork, or chicken, make sure to add lots of water to the roasting pan while the meat is cooking. Remove the roast when done and skim off the fat. Put the pan on a stove-top burner at medium heat. Put 2 Tblsp. (heaping) flour in a clean jar (plus 1 or 2 Tblsp. dry milk). Add about a cup of cold water, cap it, and shake the dickens out of it. Pour the flour mixture slowly into the simmering broth and stir constantly until thickened. (If you have a lot of liquid, you may need to use more flour.) Salt and pepper to taste. **Cost: 2¢**

> Adding flour to liquid will make it lump. Adding liquid to flour works better. Mixing the flour with a tablespoon or two of dry milk first before adding the cool liquid makes the whole process much less lumpy and frustrating.

Toasted Flour

2 cups white flour

Browned flour can be added to liquids without lumping and will serve to brown stews and sauces without additives. Place the flour in a heavy skillet. Heat over medium burner, stirring constantly. Flour will begin to brown fairly suddenly, so be sure to constantly scrape bottom and sides of skillet until flour has lightly browned evenly throughout. The thickening properties are somewhat less than regular flour so you may need to increase proportions slightly.

CAUTION—flour heated over direct heat without being stirred is EXPLOSIVE! This procedure can be very dangerous if you fail to keep the flour moving. For the same reason, never throw flour on a kitchen fire to extinguish it. Use salt, baking soda, or smother it with a lid instead.

Tuna Noodle Casserole

1 lb. noodles
8 cups water
2 6½-oz. cans tuna, drained
1 Tblsp. salt
¾ cup drained cooked peas
2 cups basic white sauce
1 bouillon cube

Cook noodles in water with 1 Tblsp. salt until tender. (The peas may be cooked with the noodles if you're starting with frozen peas.) Drain well. Add peas and tuna. Mix in white sauce to which the bouillon has been added. Bake covered at 300° for 20-30 minutes.

Cost: $2.27

Variation: In place of tuna, add 1½ cups of cubed ham. (This is a good use for leftover ham.)

Cold Tuna Pie

1 small onion chopped
1 small dill pickle, chopped
  (or 2 Tblsp. relish)
2 hard-boiled eggs, chopped
1 6½-oz. can tuna, drained
1 medium carrot, shredded
1 green (or red) pepper, shredded
1 cup cooked (leftover) rice
1 cup mayonnaise
2 Tblsp. dill pickle brine

Combine all ingredients. Spoon into prepared bread crumb crust (page 180) and chill, covered, for 1 hour.   **Cost incl. crust: $1.79**

Tuna Macaroni Salad

1 6½-oz. can tuna, drained
1 pkg. frozen mixed vegetables or leftovers
2 cups cooked macaroni, cooled
2 hard boiled eggs, chopped
2 cups mayonnaise
1½ tsp. horseradish

Steam frozen vegetables for 6-8 minutes and cool. Combine first four ingredients and toss lightly to mix. Combine mayonnaise with horseradish. Add to first four ingredients. Chill.   **Cost: $2.00**

Chicken or Turkey Salad

3 cups of diced cooked poultry
1 cup mayonnaise
1 small onion, chopped
1 dill pickle, chopped
2 hard boiled eggs, chopped
½ tsp. celery seed
½ tsp. salt
1 cup chopped celery

Combine all ingredients. Mix well. Chill.   **Cost: $2.37**

Variation: Substitute 3 cans of tuna for chicken.   **Cost: $2.61**

Squash Boats

2 winter squash (acorn, hubbard, butternut)
1 pkg. (1 lb.) lentils, cooked
½ cup salted peanuts
apple juice, lemon juice (or cooking sherry)
2 slices cooked bacon, chopped
    or 1 cup shredded cheese

Cut each squash in half and place cut-side-down on greased cookie sheet. Bake for 30 minutes at 350°. Remove from oven and scoop out seeds. Sprinkle juice or sherry in each squash cup. Add lentils mixed with peanuts and garnish with bacon or cheese. Return to oven for 20 minutes more.   **Cost: $2.37**

Scalloped Potatoes

This dish is rich in protein, so meat is not essential for serving as a main course.

4 cups of sliced potatoes
1 large onion, thinly sliced
6 Tblsp. flour
(½ cup dry milk)
3 cups milk (or enough to cover potatoes)
salt & pepper to taste
3 Tblsp. margarine
(diced ham, bacon, or sausage)

In a quart jar place the flour, (dry milk), salt and pepper. Seal and shake thoroughly. Add cold milk. Seal and shake again until all flour is dissolved. In a well-greased 3-quart casserole dish, layer the potatoes and onions, dotting each layer with margarine. Add the flour-milk mixture. Bake in a 325° oven for approximately 1½ hours.

Cost not counting meat: 67¢

Variation: for **Potato-Lentil Casserole**, substitute 1 cup lentils for half of the potatoes and increase the milk to 3½ cups.

Cost: 77¢

Variation: for **Au Gratin Potatoes**, add 1½-2 cups cubed cheese.

Cost: about $1.67

Lentil-Rice Casserole

1 cup uncooked lentils
1 cup uncooked rice
4½ cups water
2 large onions, chopped
salt & pepper to taste
(curry)
(grated cheese)

Put all ingredients (except cheese) in an ovenware dish, cover, and bake 1 hour at 350°. Serve grated cheese at the table, along with a large salad.

Cost for casserole: 73¢ + cheese

Mexicali Casserole

1 cup raw rice
1 can kidney beans (15 oz.), drained
1 can corn (not cream-style) (15 oz.), drained
1 large can crushed tomatoes (28 oz.)
2 onions, diced
2 cups water
salt, pepper, and hot sauce to taste
(cheese, yogurt, or sour cream)

Mix all ingredients in a casserole and bake, covered, for 1 hour at 350°. If you have leftover cheese ends, grate them on top. Or use the contrast of cool cottage cheese, sour cream, or yogurt as a topping if you've made it especially spicy. **Cost: about $1.97**

Welsh Rarebit

1½ cups cubed cheese (stale cheese is good)
1 cup beer
1 cup milk
2 Tblsp. flour
1 egg

Shake flour, milk, and egg in a clean jar. Place all ingredients in a pan over low heat and stir constantly. Do not let the mixture boil or the egg will curdle. Serve over toast or biscuits. Or try it on grilled tomatoes or zucchini, with biscuits on the side.
Cost: about $2.23 on toast

Macaroni and Cheese

2-3 cups of macaroni
6 quarts water
2 cups white sauce (see page 133)
1½ cups cheese cubed

Cook macaroni in 6 quarts of boiling water for 7 to 10 minutes or until tender. Drain completely. Melt the cheese completely into white sauce. Combine with cooked macaroni. If desired, add 1 cup cooked green peas or garnish with pimientos. You can use almost any kind of cheese—sharp cheddar or processed cheese loaf.
Cost: about $1.93

Spoonbread

3 cups water
1 cup cornmeal
1 cup dry milk
2 Tblsp. margarine
(grated onion)
2-3 Tblsp. oil
1 cup water
4 eggs, beaten (or 5 small)
2 tsp. baking powder
½ tsp. salt

Preheat oven to 400°. Put baking dish with oil in oven to heat. In a saucepan, mix the first four ingredients (plus grated onions) and bring to a boil, stirring constantly. When fully thickened, remove from the heat. Mix last four ingredients together quickly and stir into hot cornmeal. Pour batter into hot baking dish and return to oven. Bake for 45 minutes.   **Cost: 80¢**

Soufflé

A soufflé is really just a white or bechamel sauce flavored with anything from vanilla to cheddar cheese and spinach—with a meringue folded in. Here is a basic recipe that works well.

2 Tblsp. margarine
2 Tblsp. flour
½ tsp. salt
1 cup milk
4 eggs separated, whites whipped stiff, not dry
1 to 2 cups grated cheese
leftover cooked vegetables

Melt margarine in a saucepan, and mix in flour. Add milk and salt, and bring to a boil. It should thicken easily. Take it off the heat and add beaten egg yolks, cheese, vegetables, and any seasoning. Finally, fold in the whipped egg whites. Put the soufflé in a greased and floured casserole with high sides, in a 400° oven for 10 minutes, then lower to 350° for 20 minutes. Serve immediately.

Cost: $1.90+

Spinach Quiche

10-inch pie shell
1 egg white
1 pkg. frozen chopped spinach
4 whole eggs plus extra yolk
4 cups milk
(1 8-oz. pkg. cream cheese)
1 tsp. salt
1 clove garlic mashed
cooked bacon, chopped

Thaw and drain spinach. Line 10-inch pie pan with pie pastry. Brush with egg white. Spread spinach (and dabs of cream cheese) in pie shell. Combine eggs, milk, salt, garlic, and pour over spinach. Top with bacon. Bake at 400° for 10 minutes. Reduce heat to 350° and bake for 15 minutes longer, or until a knife inserted in the center comes out clean.   **Cost: $1.94**

Baked Fish and Vegetables

4 fresh fish fillets
4 medium potatoes—cut in 1-inch cubes
4 medium carrots—cut in 1-inch cubes
4 small onions, quartered
4 Tblsp. margarine
Salt, pepper, garlic powder, celery seed

On each of 4 squares of aluminum foil (9-inch squares) place a fish fillet and a portion of potato, carrot, and onion. Add 1 Tblsp. margarine to each square. Sprinkle with seasonings. Fold foil over and seal edges well. Bake on a cookie sheet at 350° for 45 minutes.
Cost: $1.93

Variation: "Paint" fish with garlic or curry mayonnaise and omit the margarine.

Oven Chicken

1 fryer cut up, or selected chicken parts
1 tsp. garlic powder
1 tsp. oregano
1 tsp. dried parsley
1 tsp. tarragon
½ tsp. poultry seasoning
½ tsp. paprika
¼ tsp. black pepper
2 Tblsp. margarine

Wash and arrange the chicken pieces in an oven-proof baking dish. Sprinkle with all spices. Cut margarine into 6 pieces. Arrange on top of the chicken. Bake covered in a 350° oven for 30 minutes. Remove cover and bake an additional 10 minutes. Use margarine and drippings to make gravy. Or mix 1 cup of white wine with 2 Tblsp. of corn starch; add to drippings and cook, stirring constantly until mixture begins to thicken and bubble. Add sauce to steamed broccoli or cauliflower and serve with chicken.

Cost: $3.40 at the time I did this survey, but prices have been much lower at other times.

Barbecued Chicken Wings
With Incredibly Easy Barbecue Sauce

2 lbs. chicken wings
½ cup grape (or other) jelly
½ cup catsup
garlic to taste

Mix jelly, catsup, and garlic. Spread chicken wings on a cookie sheet and spoon half or a little more of the barbecue sauce over each piece. Bake in a 350° oven for 20 minutes. Turn and baste with remaining sauce. Bake for another 20 minutes. (Goes well with Oven-fried Potatoes, page 158.)   **Cost for barbecue sauce: 31¢
Cost for chicken wings: $1.89 or less**

Turkey Burgers

½ lb. ground turkey
1 egg
¼ cup dry oatmeal
2 Tblsp. catsup
½ medium onion, finely chopped
(4 slices Swiss cheese)
¼ cup mayonnaise
1 Tblsp. horseradish
½ tsp. garlic powder

Combine turkey, egg, oatmeal, onion, catsup, and garlic powder and make into patties. Cook in a greased skillet until brown. Flip and place one slice of cheese on each burger. Mix mayonnaise and horseradish and spread on rye bread or bun. Makes 4 burgers.

Cost for burgers: $1.04

Pizza

4 cups flour
1 package yeast (1 Tblsp.)
1¼ cup luke-warm water
1 tsp. salt
2 Tblsp. oil
1 large can tomato sauce
1 8-oz. pkg. mozzarella cheese (grated)
1 large onion, chopped
½ cup mushrooms

Mix yeast in water as for bread. Add flour and salt and mix. Knead for 10 minutes, then let rise. Stretch the dough over a cookie sheet, making sure to turn up the edges. Spread with the tomato sauce, then sprinkle on grated cheese, mushrooms, and onions. Put in 400° oven and cook for about half an hour. (You can make two at once and freeze the second. It should keep at least a week.)

Cost: $2.68

Quick Lasagna

1 box lasagna noodles
1 large jar spaghetti sauce
1 1-lb. carton cottage cheese
1 8-oz. pkg. mozzarella cheese (grated)
2 eggs, beaten
3 cloves garlic, mashed
salt & pepper to taste
1 pkg. frozen chopped spinach, thawed

Mix eggs, cottage cheese, spinach, and spices. Grease lasagna pan. Spread tomato sauce thickly on bottom and add one layer of *uncooked* noodles. Do not overlap. Spread ½ of the egg and cheese mix on top; sprinkle with ½ of mozzarella. Cover with tomato sauce and repeat, finishing with tomato sauce. Bake, *covered* with foil, for 1 hour at 350°. **Cost: $4.93**

Vegetarian Chili

2 cans kidney beans (15 oz.)
1 cup or so cooked rice
1 large can crushed tomatoes (28 oz.)
1 tomato-can of water
1 large onion, diced
1 clove garlic, crushed
1 Tblsp. chili powder
dash of hot sauce

When you have leftover rice, this meal is a snap. Combine all ingredients, except rice, and simmer for 30 minutes. Add rice 5 minutes before serving. **Cost: $1.89**

Spaghetti Sauce

Ground beef (up to 1 lb.)
1 medium onion, chopped,
1 can mushrooms, stems & pieces
1 large can tomato sauce (28 oz.)
1 small can tomato paste
2 small cans water
salt & pepper to taste
bay leaf
garlic
oregano
tarragon

Brown meat and combine all ingredients. Cook covered over a low heat for several hours, stirring occasionally. Serve over pasta.

Cost, including 1 lb. pasta: $3.88

Variation: for **Meatless Spaghetti,** use 1 cup of lentils instead of ground beef, but increase the water by 1 cup.

Cost, including 1 lb. pasta: $2.53

Variation: Ground turkey is a good beef substitute and less greasy. It is usually less expensive, too.

Bolognese Spaghetti Sauce

½ lb. hamburger
1 small onion
1 small carrot, diced
1 small celery stalk, diced
1 can crushed tomatoes (28 oz.)
¼ cup red wine
¼ cup milk
1 Tblsp. vegetable oil
rosemary
salt & pepper to taste

Brown meat and vegetables in oil. Add rosemary and cook over moderate heat, then add tomatoes, wine, and milk. The milk makes all the difference. Serve over pasta.

Cost, including 1 lb. pasta: $2.82

147

Noodles Stroganoff

I normally do not cook with condensed soup. But recipe is special, and, for a carry-in dinner after work, incredibly quick.

> 1 lb. noodles
> 1 can condensed beef soup
> 1 can golden mushroom soup
> ½ soup-can-full red wine or beef bouillon
> 1 3-oz. can mushroom pieces, drained
> 1 8-oz. container sour cream
> (leftover meat, diced)

Cook the noodles until tender in 6 quarts of boiling salted water. Drain well. Combine soups with wine or bouillon. Add mushrooms. Heat thoroughly. Add sour cream. Pour over the noodles. Toss to combine. **Cost, not counting meat: $3.73**

Beef and Noodles

This recipe takes no longer to prepare than a commercial "Helper" package. Furthermore, you would get only six ounces of noodles in one of those boxes.

> 1 lb. hamburger
> ¼ cup flour
> salt & pepper to taste
> 1 tsp. garlic powder
> dash of "hot" sauce
> 1 lb. uncooked noodles
> 6 cups water

Brown the meat. Add spices, water, and bring to a boil. Add noodles. Cook until the noodles are tender, about 10 minutes. Shake flour in a jar with ½ cup water. Add to the broth and stir constantly until thickened. Use hot sauce to taste. **Cost incl. meat: $2.37**
Cost of a "Helper" plus meat: $3.46

Variation: With (leftover) veggies, this becomes a complete, one-dish meal.

For chicken or turkey and noodles, cook poultry in salted water until completely tender. Remove the meat from the bones and return to the stock. Add noodles and cook as above.

"Steak" and Mushroom Gravy

½ onion, chopped
5 Tblsp. toasted flour, page 136
2 cups water
5 Tblsp. dry milk
1 Tblsp. margarine
1-2 cups leftover beef
1 small can mushroom pieces
salt & pepper to taste
(1 mushroom-can-full of red wine)

Melt margarine in a large skillet and sauté onion. Mix flour, seasoning, and dry milk in a jar. Add water and shake. Stir into onions until simmering and thickened. Add beef and drained mushrooms. Reduce the heat. Simmer, stirring constantly until heated through. Serve over noodles, rice, or mashed potatoes.

Cost, not counting meat: 90¢

Shepherd's Pie

¾ lb. hamburger (or leftover meat)
1 large onion, diced (or onion soup mix)
1 lb. frozen green beans (or other veggie)
2 Tblsp. flour
1 cup water
6 potatoes, cooked and mashed
salt and pepper

Take frozen vegetable out of the freezer to thaw (or thaw in microwave). Peel potatoes and dice in small pieces to speed cooking. Scramble hamburger in frying pan with onion. Drain fat when done. Shake flour and water together in a jar and add to the pan, stirring until thickened. Spread veggie layer on top. Mash potatoes and mound on top of the meat-vegetable mixture, spreading out to the edge of the pan. Sprinkle with seasoned salt or paprika. Bake at 350° for 30 minutes.

Cost: $2.70

Meat loaf is an expression of individual personality. You can put in anything from peanut butter to green beans. Here are my two favorites.

Tomato Meat Loaf

2 lbs. ground beef
1 medium onion, chopped
1 egg
1 small can tomato paste
¾ cup dry oatmeal
salt & pepper to taste

Combine all ingredients and bake in a loaf pan at 350° for 50-60 minutes.

Cost: $3.93

Mushroom Meat Loaf

2 lbs. ground beef
1 medium onion, chopped
1 egg
½ can cream of mushroom soup
1 small can mushroom stems & pieces
⅓ cup oatmeal (or cracker crumbs)
salt (omit if using crackers)
pepper

Combine all ingredients and bake in a loaf pan at 350° for 50-60 minutes.

Cost: $4.32

To keep the sides of a meat loaf tender, set the loaf pan in a larger pan filled with water.

Ham and Vegetable Pot

1 ham bone (1-1½ lbs.)
6-8 cups water
4 potatoes, diced
2 cups coarsely chopped cabbage
1 lb. frozen green beans or corn
salt & pepper to taste

Bring the water to a boil. Add salt and ham bone. Reduce the heat to a simmer. Cook for several hours, until the meat comes off the bone. If necessary, add water during cooking. Add vegetables for the last half hour of cooking. Dip meat and vegetables out to serve.

Cost: $3.08

Hot Dog and Sauerkraut Casserole

1½ lb. bag or can sauerkraut
10 hot dogs, whole or cut-up
¼ tsp. caraway seeds
1 cup beer

Drain the sauerkraut. Place sauerkraut and beer in an oven-proof dish with a lid and steam in a 350° oven for 15 minutes. Add the franks and caraway seeds and steam another 15 minutes.

Cost: $1.44

151

Polish Casserole

1 small kielbasa sausage (½ lb. or so)
1 can cannellini white beans (15 oz.)
1 can kidney beans (15 oz.)
2 Tblsp. margarine
¼ cup flour
1½ cup cold water
½ cup dry milk
salt & pepper (lots)

You need very little of the kielbasa to flavor this casserole and any mix of cooked beans will do, including limas, chick peas, navy beans, etc. Melt margarine in a frying pan. Add flour and mix to paste consistency. Shake water and dry milk in a jar and add quickly to the pan, stirring constantly as it thickens. Season to taste. Drain beans and place in a 1-quart casserole with sliced kielbasa. Cover with cream sauce and bake in 350° oven for 30 minutes.

Cost: $2.41

Stuffed Cabbage

8 cabbage leaves
1½ lbs. ground turkey
1 large onion, chopped
1½ cups cooked rice
1 small can tomato paste
½ tsp. garlic powder
1 large can tomato sauce (28 oz.)
1 sauce-can of water
salt & pepper to taste

Soak the cabbage leaves in boiling water for 2 to 3 minutes to soften. Combine meat, onion, rice, tomato paste, salt, pepper, and garlic powder. Place approximately ½ cup of the meat mixture into the cup of the cabbage leaf. Fold both sides of the leaf over the meat mixture. Roll to the tip of the leaf. Secure with toothpicks and place in large frying pan. Combine tomato sauce with water and pour over cabbage rolls. Cook uncovered until sauce boils. Reduce the heat and cover. Simmer for at least 1½ hours, stirring sauce occasionally. Serves 8, or freeze the extra. **Cost: $3.17**

Autumn Casserole

½ small head cabbage, shredded
3 apples, cored and diced
2 onions, diced
1 cup raisins
1 lb. container cottage cheese
1 cup raw rice
½ cup peanut butter
2 cups water
dash nutmeg

Bring water to a boil and add the shredded cabbage. Turn off burner and let sit for 5 minutes, while you fix the apples and onions. Pour off ½ cup of the hot water and add the peanut butter. Blend well and set aside. Place all other ingredients in the casserole—layered or mixed—including the cabbage water. (Replace with fresh water if you want to downplay the cabbage flavor.) Pour the peanut butter gravy on top and cover. Bake at 350° for 1 hour.

Cost: $3.47

Sausage and Rice Casserole

1 cup raw rice
½ lb. sausage, browned
2 onions, diced (or 1 pkg. of onion soup mix)
1 lb. of frozen peas or veggie of choice
2 cups water

Use cut-up links or scrambled bulk sausage, with fat drained. Then add sausage and vegetable to rice. Bake at 350° for 1 hour.

Cost: $2.43

Variation: **Chicken Rice Casserole**—substitute 1 cup of minced chicken or chicken parts for sausage.

Stir Fry

2 cups shredded cabbage
2 onions, sliced
2 green peppers, sliced
2 stalks celery, sliced
1 cup turnip, peeled and diced or shredded
1 cup (or less) of leftover meat or chicken
3-4 slices ginger root, peeled and minced
2 cloves garlic, mashed
1 Tblsp. oil
2 Tblsp. or so water
2 Tblsp. soy sauce
1 Tblsp. cornstarch (or 2 Tblsp. flour)
3 Tblsp. peanut butter
½ tsp. hot sauce (or red pepper oil)
1 cup water

In a deep skillet, simmer the oil with ginger and garlic over medium heat. Add vegetables—starting with the firmest—as you dice the others (vary to suit your taste—broccoli or summer squash are nice, too). Stir after each addition and sprinkle on water (or oil) as needed. Do not overcook! Add cooked meat last thing. Mix peanut butter, soy sauce, hot sauce, and cornstarch in 1 cup water. Push vegetables to the side and add sauce to the pot while stirring. Add additional water, if needed. As sauce clears, mix in vegetables. Serve over rice. **Cost, counting rice but not leftover meat: $2.45**

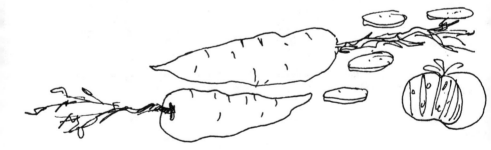

Company Fondue

There are so many variations of the fondue theme that you ought to check the library for a fondue cookbook. Or just let your imagination take over. Many people don't know what to do with a fondue set, so the chances are good you'll be able to snag a cast-off wedding present—cheap—at a garage sale.

One reason this meal is ideal for company is that it allows you to pick what you can afford while including a wide variety of foods, and there's bound to be something to please everyone. Kids—if they're not too young—enjoy this meal, too, because it keeps them active. And for someone trying to lose weight, the leisurely pace gives your brain a chance to say "full" before you've gorged yourself.

I'll price this meal without including the optional items (the ones in parentheses). You could blow your budget if you're not careful. But if you have to impress the boss or a prospective mother-in-law, here's how! The flexibility of ingredients will allow you to choose from low-cost in-season veggies, too, so you may be able to do it for less than the prices quoted here.

1 chicken breast, skinned and boned
1 cube steak (or other steak)—about ½ lb.
(½ lb. frozen shrimp, cooked and peeled)
(½ lb. scallops)
1 small zucchini or summer squash
1 green pepper
(1 red and 1 yellow pepper)
1 sweet potato, peeled
1 white potato, peeled
(3 Jerusalem artichokes, peeled)
1 stalk fresh broccoli (and/or cauliflower)
(1 pkg. frozen brussels sprouts, thawed)
(1 pint cherry tomatoes)
(4 spears asparagus—in season)
(½ lb. fresh mushrooms)
(1 bunch scallions)
1 pkg. onion soup mix
2-3 cups water
(2½ cups vegetable oil)

Cut everything that isn't already bite-sized—or nearly so—into manageable sizes and arrange in groups on a large platter. If you are having a large crowd, you might want to make two platters—a meat (and seafood) platter and a veggie platter or two combination plates. Scallions make an attractive divider between groups. Cover with a wet paper towel or plastic wrap and keep in the refrigerator until dinnertime.   **Cost: $5.01+**

Sauces

Now it's time to make the sauces, the more the merrier, if you can find enough small dishes in which to serve them. **Curried Mayo** (page 182), **Garlic Mayo** (page 181), and **Incredibly Easy Barbecue Sauce** (page 144) are good for starters. For a cocktail sauce, mix catsup with horseradish. (If you're stout-hearted, try an anchovy-mustard sauce: mix mashed anchovies with an equal amount of grey mustard and thin with a bit of oil and vinegar. Chopped chives or parsley will give it color.) Or a plain grey mustard dip is just fine. A cheap creamy dip (page 181) is a nice addition, too, especially if you don't want to go to the trouble of making something extravagant like a Béarnaise sauce. (Or you could cheat with a "ranch" dressing if you're desperate for time.)

Cost: Add another 50¢, at least

In your fondue pot, heat the onion soup mix and water on the stove before bringing to the table. (If you need a second pot or want to use the oil-cooking method, heat that ahead, too.) Keep the pots hot over Sterno.   **Cost for one small can Sterno: $1.00**

And if you're really putting on the dog, prepare the cheese fondue that follows, and keep three pots going. That way, you can cook meat in the oil, veggies in the onion soup, and dip anything you feel like in the cheese. Or you could skip the meat and seafood, and use just the cheese and onion soup. By the way, it's always permissible to nosh on raw veggies while you're waiting for something to cook.

Cheese Fondue

1 lb. cheese, cubed
2 Tblsp. flour
2 cups milk
  (or trade ½ cupful for wine or beer)
nutmeg to taste
dash hot sauce
1 loaf of French bread, cubed
  (or 4 English muffins)

You will probably want to experiment with types of cheese, but even the less expensive ones such as Monterey Jack will do just fine. Mix milk and flour in a jar and shake to blend. Add everything to the fondue pot on your stove and stir while heating over low-medium heat. The smaller the pieces of cheese, the more quickly they will melt into the sauce as it thickens. Transfer to the table and keep warm over a *low* Sterno fire. While French bread is more traditional with this meal, kids especially will find the firm pieces of English muffin easier to handle. (Serve with a salad or combine with a vegetable platter as mentioned earlier.)　**Cost for Sterno: $1.00**
For fondue: $3.32+

Chocolate Fondue

Even though this probably should have been saved for the dessert section, if you're having an evening of fondue this is the perfect way to end it. Definitely not cheap, but well worth saving money on other meals so you can splurge once in a while!

1 pkg. semi-sweet baking chocolate
½ cup strong coffee
½ cup coffee cream ("Half & Half")
1 small can mandarin oranges
1 small jar maraschino cherries
1 small can pineapple bits
(½ cup walnut halves)

Heat coffee, cream, and broken chocolate pieces over low heat while stirring. Transfer to the table and keep warm over a candle burner. Try fresh fruit in season (grapes, strawberries, etc.) or even mini-marshmallows.　**Cost: $5.36**

Side Dishes

Rice

Melt 2 Tblsp. of margarine in an oven-proof, 3-quart sauce pan with a lid. Add and brown slightly 1 cup of raw rice. Add 2 cups of water, stir, and cover immediately. Turn the heat way down, and don't touch it for 15 minutes. At the end of that time, *without removing the lid,* put the casserole into a 350° oven for another 15 minutes. If you're not using the oven for other dinner preparations, this could be finished on top of the stove, but the oven method is best. Rice can be flavored with any herbs plus a bouillon cube for a considerable saving over packaged rice specialties. **Cost: 31¢**

Potato Pancakes I

1-1½ cups leftover mashed potatoes
1 egg
¼ cup milk
¼ cup flour
2 tsp. baking powder
½ tsp. salt
½ onion, finely chopped

Mix the potatoes with egg, milk, and onion. Sift together flour, baking powder, and salt. Add to potato mixture. Fry on a greased griddle as for pancakes. Serve with apple sauce, sour cream, cheese sauce, or meat and mushroom gravy.

Cost without leftover mashed potatoes: 22¢
Applesauce topping: 25¢

Potato Pancakes II

4 medium to large potatoes, washed
1 large onion
1 egg
salt & pepper to taste

Grate raw potatoes and onion. Mix with egg, salt, and pepper (lots, if you like pepper). Fry on a greased griddle. **Cost: 31¢**

Variation: add whole corn kernels to either recipe.

Potatoes Galette

4 potatoes, thinly sliced
4 Tblsp. margarine

Melt margarine in a frying pan; layer the slices in the pan, then cook over a medium heat. Shake the pan while cooking until the potatoes are a golden brown.   **Cost: 20¢**

Oven-fried Potatoes

4 potatoes, thinly sliced
4 Tblsp. or so vegetable oil
garlic powder

Rub each potato slice with oil. Spread out on cookie sheet and sprinkle with garlic powder. Bake at 325° for 30 minutes. **Cost: 30¢**

Stuffing

Stuffing is something of an expression of individual personality. But here are some suggestions that are less expensive and tastier than the pre-packaged commercial varieties.

2 Tblsp. margarine
1 onion, chopped
2 tsp. sage
2 tsp. garlic powder or 2 cloves of garlic
8 cups dried bread cubes or cubed toast
4 cups chicken stock or prepared bouillon

Melt margarine in a 1-quart sauce pan and sauté the onion. Add sage and garlic. (A clove of garlic is *not* a bulb. The bulb is about the size of a ping pong ball and is made up of several cloves.) To the onions and seasoning, add bread cubes. Toss lightly. Then add poultry stock or bouillon. The bread will seem to melt but should hold its form. Use to stuff a chicken or turkey, or bake in a greased casserole dish covered for 35-40 minutes at 350°.   **Cost: 34¢**

Variation: Add ½ to 1 cup chopped celery, 1-1½ cups sliced mushrooms, 1-2 cups chopped cooked poultry, or, if you're feeling rich or live on the coast, a pint of oysters. Cooked sausage or bacon with raisins and nuts are nice variations, too.

Cornmeal Loaf

With cheese sauce, this has enough protein to serve as a light supper rather than a side dish. With applesauce, it's a warm winter breakfast.

3 cups boiling water
1 cup cold water
1 cup cornmeal
¼ cup flour
1 tsp. salt
½ cup dry milk
1 onion, finely chopped

Boil 3 cups of water in double boiler top. Mix cornmeal with all other ingredients in cold water and add slowly, stirring constantly as it thickens. Put top of double boiler over bottom part and cook over hot water for 30 minutes more, covered. Pour into a loaf pan and cool. When firm, slice and fry in a greased pan. **Cost: 52¢**

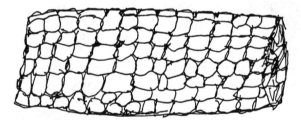

One-eyed Egyptian Sandwich

1 egg per person
1 slice of bread each
margarine

Butter the bread. Then, using a cookie cutter or glass, cut a hole out of the center. Put both pieces of bread in the frying pan, buttered side down. Break an egg into the hole of the large piece. (This is a great use for those little eggs that come in boxes of 2½ dozen.) Butter the top sides and flip. **Cost per serving: 8¢**

Barbecued Onions

6 medium onions
6 bouillon cubes
3 Tblsp. margarine
pepper to taste

Peel onions. Scoop out a hole in the top of each onion. Fill with bouillon cube, ½ tsp. margarine, and pepper. Wrap separately in foil. Place on barbecue grill, turning frequently, for 30 minutes.

Cost: 45¢

Baked Onion Slices

4 large onions, peeled and sliced
¼ cup vinegar
¼ cup sugar
¼ cup melted margarine
¼ cup boiling water

Arrange onions in a casserole. Combine other ingredients. Pour over onions, and bake at 300° for 1 hour.

Cost: 53¢

Baked Onions

Place unpeeled onions in a pie tin or other pan to catch the juice. Bake for about 30 minutes. Time and temperature can be adjusted to accommodate other baking needs.

Cost: about 5¢ per onion

Fried Apples and Onions

½ lb. sliced bacon
6 medium onions
6 medium apples
2 Tblsp. brown sugar

Cook bacon and remove from skillet. Reserve 2 Tblsp. of fat. Peel and thinly slice onions. Core and slice apples (no need to peel). In reserved bacon fat, cook onions over medium heat for 6-7 minutes. Cover evenly with apple slices; top with brown sugar. Cover. Cook until tender, approximately 5 minutes. Serve with bacon.

Cost: $2.01

Pineapple and Beets

2 16-oz. cans sliced beets, drained
1 can pineapple chunks
⅓ cup vinegar
1 Tblsp. cornstarch
¼ cup sugar

Drain pineapple, reserving syrup. In a medium saucepan combine cornstarch, salt, and sugar. Blend in pineapple syrup, vinegar, and water. Cook over medium heat, stirring constantly, until mixture thickens. Add beets and pineapple. Heat thoroughly.

Cost: $2.29

Creamed Beets

24 small beets, cooked or canned
¼ cup vinegar
2 Tblsp. water
½ stick margarine (¼ cup)
⅔ cup sour cream

Combine vinegar, water, and margarine in a medium saucepan. Bring to a boil and add beets, sliced or whole. Heat through. Add sour cream last.

Cost: $1.76

Candied Carrots

½ lb. fresh carrots
½ stick margarine
¼ cup brown sugar
2 tsp. cinnamon

Clean carrots and cut into bite-size pieces. Steam 10 minutes or just until tender. Melt margarine in a large skillet over low heat. Add sugar and cinnamon. Cook 1-2 minutes. Add hot carrots, stirring well to coat.

Cost: 41¢

Carrot Casserole

6 carrots, sliced
8 medium apples, sliced
½ stick margarine
salt

Layer apples and carrots in a greased casserole. Sprinkle each layer with salt. Cut margarine into pieces. Arrange on top. Bake covered at 350° for 45 minutes. **Cost: $1.31**

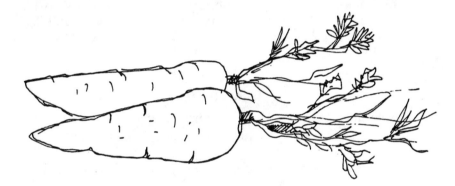

Fried Green Tomatoes

½ cup vegetable oil
4-6 medium unpeeled green tomatoes, sliced
1 cup flour
2 quarts of water
2 Tblsp. salt

Soak sliced tomatoes in salt water mixture for 30-40 minutes. Drain and drop slices a few at a time into a bag in which you have placed the flour. Shake thoroughly to coat.

Heat the oil in a large skillet and carefully place the slices into the hot oil. Brown until crisp on both sides. Salt to taste. These are great in a sandwich with mustard, too! *Variation:* substitute zucchini, squash, cucumbers, or eggplant for the green tomatoes. **Cost: $1.28**

Wilted Cabbage

1 onion, sliced
several apples—peeled, cored, and sliced
½ small red cabbage, chopped
2 Tblsp. oil

Sauté onion in oil or bacon fat. Add remaining ingredients. Stir occasionally over low heat, add water if necessary to keep moist. Cook until tender (about 15 to 30 minutes). **Cost: $1.15**

Variations: For **Chinese Cabbage** (bok choi)—add ½ to 1 tsp. ginger shortly before cabbage is done. For **Sweet and Sour Cabbage**—add 1 Tblsp. vinegar and 1 Tblsp. dark brown sugar prior to cooking.

Gnocchi Verdi

This side dish has enough protein to serve without meat.

1 small onion, peeled and chopped
1 Tblsp. margarine
1 pkg. frozen chopped spinach, thawed
¾ cup cottage cheese
1 egg, beaten
1 cup parmesan cheese
⅔ cup flour
salt, pepper, & nutmeg to taste
1 chicken bouillon cube dissolved in
2 cups hot water

Sauté onion and spinach in margarine. Mix the next five ingredients in a bowl and add spinach and onions. Flour hands and shape into walnut-size balls. Simmer balls in broth for 3-4 minutes. Keep warm until serving time. **Cost: about $2.50**

Soups and Stews

Vegetable Beef Soup

1 beef soup bone
    or 1 lb. stewing beef, cut small
6-8 cups water
2-4 cups potatoes, cubed
1 cup sliced carrots
1 cup green beans
1 cup corn
½ cup coarsely chopped onion
1-2 cups tomatoes, chopped
1-2 cups cabbage, chopped
½ cup barley, split peas, or rice

Brown beef in a frying pan if you are using fresh meat. Then add meat or bone to cold water with potatoes. Bring to a boil and add the other vegetables. Add barley, rice, or split peas. Reduce to a simmer. Add salt, pepper, garlic, bay leaf, tarragon or any spices or herbs you are comfortable using. (Remove the meat from the bones when it begins to leave the bone or pull away. Chop the beef and return it to the soup.) When cold, remove any congealed fat from the top and discard.   **Cost with soup bone: $3.70**
Cost with stewing beef: $5.00

Potato Soup

3 medium potatoes, cubed
1 onion, grated
1 bay leaf
salt & pepper to taste
1 cup dry milk
4 Tblsp. flour
4 cups cold water

Blend flour, milk powder, and part of the water in a jar. Add all ingredients to the pot and bring to a simmer, stirring occasionally.
Cost: 46¢

Chicken Stew

1 frying or stewing hen, or chicken parts
water to cover
4 potatoes, diced
4 carrots, sliced
4 onions, peeled
1-2 stalks celery, diced
thyme
salt & pepper to taste
3 or more Tblsp. flour
½ cup cold water

Add whole chicken, vegetables, and seasoning to pot of water. Bring to a boil and simmer, covered, for 1½ hours or until meat is done. Remove all meat from the bones, chop the chicken, and return it to the stock. (Or you can cut portions off when serving and bone it later for leftovers. However, you can stretch a chicken if you do the cutting first.) To thicken stock, shake flour and ½ cup cold water in a jar. Stir into simmering stock until thickened.

Cost: $2.82

Variation: **Chicken and Dumplings**—omit potatoes and cook dumplings in stew after chicken and vegetables are nearly tender. Thicken after dumplings are removed if necessary. **Cost: $2.90**

Chicken Noodle Soup—omit the potatoes and thickening. After boning the chicken, add a 1-lb. package of noodles to boiling stock. Cook for 10 minutes more. **Cost: $3.12**

Turkey Chowder

1 lb. ground or leftover turkey
2 onions, chopped
1 slice of bacon, diced or crumbled
4 potatoes, diced
1 pkg. frozen corn or canned corn
6-8 cups water
1 cup powdered milk
salt & pepper to taste
thyme
sage

Sauté bacon and onions. Add turkey and brown, if using fresh turkey. Transfer to soup pot and add remaining ingredients. Simmer on medium-low heat for 1½ hours or until potatoes are tender.

Cost with ground turkey: $2.17
Cost with leftover turkey: 98¢

Nickel-bone Soup

1 turkey carcass
2 Tblsp. vinegar
water to cover
2 cups barley
4 carrots, sliced
3 stalks celery, diced
3 onions, diced
1 can tomatoes (28 oz.)
salt & pepper to taste

Simmer carcass in pot of water and vinegar for 1-2 hours. (Vinegar draws calcium from the bones, I'm told, and tenderizes any tough parts.) Lift out and cool enough to handle. Put rescued meat (and perhaps a bone or two) back in the pot with all other ingredients—except tomatoes—and cook 1 hour more. Add tomatoes during last 10 minutes. Kids get a nickel for every bone they find at dinner.

Cost (plus nickels): $2.25

167

Split Pea Soup

1 ham bone (or 2 slices cooked bacon)
1 lb. split or whole dried peas
1 large onion, grated
2 carrots, grated
8 cups water
salt to taste & lots of pepper

Toss all ingredients in a pot and bring to a boil. Reduce heat and simmer for 2 hours, covered. Remove bone and cut any remaining meat away. Dice and return to soup.   **Cost: about 74¢**

Variation: **Bean Soup**—Sort and soak the dried beans (use any available variety) in water overnight. Water should be about 2 inches over the beans to allow for swelling. Drain, rinse, and add 8 more cups of water. Then follow above directions.

Tomato Soup

1 28-oz. can broken or crushed tomatoes
   or 2-4 fresh tomatoes
1 small onion, grated
1 bay leaf
1 tsp. sugar
salt & pepper to taste
½ cup dry milk
2 Tblsp. flour
1½ cups cold water

Smash the tomatoes and cook with onion, bay leaf, sugar, salt, and pepper for 10-15 minutes. Remove the bay leaf and put the tomato mixture through a sieve or strainer to remove the seeds and skin. In a covered jar or shaker, combine the flour and dry milk and shake well. Add the cold water and shake again to dissolve. Put the milk and flour mixture in the now empty pan and cook until thickened, stirring constantly. Add the strained tomatoes back in and cook for 10 minutes, stirring constantly.   **Cost: 84¢**

Green Bean Soup

2 cans green beans
½ medium onion
1 tsp. lemon juice
½ cup flour
½ stick margarine (¼ cup)
2 cups milk
1 cup cold water
1 Tblsp. soy sauce
    or instant bouillon
salt & pepper to taste

Cook beans until tender, drain, puree in blender or food processor with onion and lemon juice. Melt margarine in a sauce pan. Blend in flour. Add milk, water, and soy or bouillon. Stir until thickened. Add pureed bean mixture; salt and pepper to taste.

Cost: $1.46

Minestrone

2 carrots
1 large onion
½ cup wax beans
1 large potato
1 can crushed tomatoes
    or 1 Tblsp. tomato paste
(rind of parmesan cheese)
3 Tblsp. oil

Chop and sauté carrots, onion, beans and potato in the oil. Add 5 cups of water, (parmesan rinds), and tomato. Let simmer for 1 hour.

Cost: $1.27

Gazpacho

This is a great way to deal with an exploding garden come July and August.

1 small onion
1 large cucumber
1 small bell pepper
3 peeled and diced tomatoes
⅓ cup oil
⅓ cup vinegar
1 cup tomato juice
2 cloves garlic
2 Tblsp. lemon juice
2 Tblsp. honey
¼ tsp. pepper
1 tsp. mayonnaise
1 tsp. dill

Put all ingredients in a blender and turn on until liquid. Chill.
Cost with store-purchased veggies: $2.65

Variation: for **Tomato Aspic,** omit oil, mayonnaise, and vinegar. Dissolve 1 envelope of unflavored gelatin in the tomato juice. Heat in microwave to dissolve. Mix with the rest of the juiced vegetables and refrigerate in 8 x 8-inch pan or mold. **Cost: $2.57**

Baked Goods

Making Your Own Mixes

In today's supermarkets, mixes are everywhere. They're great because they're easy, they're self-contained, and they're fast. Just add a couple of items, mix, and you're in business. They do, however, have a few drawbacks. The main one is, of course, that they're expensive. Any time you don't have to measure, mix, and package, you are paying someone else to do it for you. The other drawback is that in prepared, or semi-prepared foods, the additives and chemicals included are often more than you really want.

Your alternatives are either to start from scratch every time you want to prepare something, or to make your own mixes.

All-purpose Baking Mix

Note: The amount in this mix is for about 5 batches of use.

> 10 cups sifted flour
> 3⅓ cups powdered milk
> 5 Tblsp. baking powder
> 2½ tsp. salt

Combine well and store in a covered container.   **Cost: $1.45**

For **Pancakes**—Combine 2¼ cups baking mix with a mixture of 1 egg, 1½ cups water, and 2 Tblsp. of vegetable oil. Stir until moistened. Your batter should be lumpy. Cook on a hot, greased griddle. Flip when bubbles break on the surface and the edges begin to dry.
Cost: 38¢

For **Dumplings**—Combine 2 cups baking mix with 1 cup of water (and spices or shredded cheese). Stir until mixed. Drop by spoonfuls into simmering soup or gravy. Cover and cook (without peeking) for 20 minutes.   **Cost: 24¢**

171

For **Biscuits**—Combine 2¼ cups baking mix with ¼ cup shortening and ⅔ cup water. Mix lightly until dough forms a ball. Turn onto a lightly floured surface. Knead 10 or 12 strokes. Roll dough about ½-inch thick. Cut with a 2-inch cutter or juice glass. Bake on an ungreased baking sheet at 450° for 10 to 12 minutes. For drop sheet biscuits, use 1 cup water and drop by Tblsp. onto baking sheet.

Cost: 35¢

For **Muffins**—Combine 2¼ cups baking mix with ¼ cup of sugar. Combine 1 egg, and ¾ cup water, with ⅓ cup vegetable oil. Add to dry ingredients. You may also add raisins, nuts, cinnamon, chopped fruit (or even veggies such as carrots or squash) for variety. Mix only enough to moisten flour, even if the batter is lumpy. Use greased or nonstick muffin pans and fill two-thirds full. (Or fill the cup only half-way, add jelly, and top with more batter.) Bake at 400° for 45 minutes.

Cost: 50¢

Streusel Coffee Cake Mix

Note: The amount in this mix should make 5 coffee cakes.

7½ cups flour
2½ tsp. salt
3¾ cups sugar
10 tsp. baking powder

Combine the above ingredients and store in covered container.

Streusel Topping Mix

1¼ cups brown sugar
10 tsp. cinnamon
1¼ cups flour
5 Tblsp. soft margarine

Combine dry ingredients. Cut in margarine until crumbly. Store, covered, in refrigerator. **Cost for cake and topping mix: $2.70**

For **Streusel Coffee Cake**—Combine 2½ cups mix with a mixture of ¼ cup vegetable oil, 1 beaten egg, and ½ cup milk. Spread into greased 8 x 8-inch pan. Top with the streusel topping mix above (approximately ¾ cup per recipe). Bake at 375° for 25 minutes.

Cost: 54¢

Breakfast Muffin Cake

If you don't like to wash muffin pans, here's an answer. Heat oven to 350°.

> 2 eggs
> 4 Tblsp. oil
> ½ cup molasses
> 2 cups water
> 1 cup dry milk
> 2 cups dry oatmeal
> 2½ cups flour
> 1 tsp. salt
> 2 tsp. baking powder
> 2 tsp. baking soda
> (raisins or a couple of tablespoons marmalade)
> (½ cup applesauce, cooked squash, carrots)

Beat wet ingredients together. Mix dry ingredients well and add, stirring only enough to blend. Bake in greased 9 x 12-inch pan for 15 minutes. Should last for two breakfasts.   **Cost: $1.65**

Zucchini Bread

> 3 eggs
> 2 cups sugar
> 1 cup oil
> 2 cups grated zucchini
> 3 cups flour
> 1 tsp. soda
> 1¼ tsp. baking powder
> ½ tsp. salt
> 1 Tblsp. cinnamon
> 1 Tblsp. vanilla
> (½ cup raisins)

Pour into 2 greased loaf pans. Bake 1 hour at 325°.
          Cost, not including zucchini: $1.60

Golden Corn Bread

2 cups yellow or white cornmeal
2 cups flour
½ cup sugar
2 Tblsp. + 2 tsp. baking powder
1 tsp. salt
2 eggs
½ cup vegetable oil
2 cups milk

Mix all together and pour into a large greased pan. (Iron skillets are supposed to work the best, but you may need two.) Bake at 450° for 25 to 30 minutes or until tested done.   **Cost: $1.43**

Bagels

2 packages dry yeast
⅔ cup warm water

4 cups flour
¾ cup water
3 Tblsp. sugar
1 Tblsp. salt

4 quarts water
1 tsp. sugar

Dissolve yeast in warm water. Add 2 cups flour, the ¾ cup water, sugar, and salt. Mix ingredients on high speed of electric mixer for 2 minutes. Reduce speed and slowly add 2 more cups of flour. When the dough becomes stiff, turn onto a floured board and knead by hand until smooth (or use a dough hook). Place in a lightly greased bowl. Cover, to rest for 15 minutes. Divide dough into 12 balls. Pierce the center of each ball to make the center hole. Pull to enlarge. Let rise, covered, for 30 minutes on a lightly greased baking sheet. Bring the 4 quarts of water to a boil. Add 1 tsp. of sugar (this aids browning). Reduce heat to simmer and add 4 bagels. After 3 minutes, turn and simmer 4 minutes longer. Remove. Pat dry and place on a lightly greased baking sheet. Repeat with the remaining bagels. Bake at 375° for 30 minutes.   **Cost: $1.14**

Fast Pretzels

A wonderful rainy-day activity to share with young children.

1 package yeast (1 Tblsp.)
4 cups flour
½ tsp. sugar
1⅓ cups warm water
1 tsp. table salt
1 egg, beaten
coarse salt (or onion flakes)

Dissolve yeast in warm water. Add flour and salt, kneading as necessary to mix in flour. Let rise in a greased bowl until doubled. Pinch off pieces and roll into 12-inch strings. Tie into knots. Brush with egg and sprinkle with coarse salt. Bake at 350° for 15-20 minutes.   **Cost: 69¢**

Bread

2 pkgs. dry yeast
7 cups flour
1 cup dry milk powder
4 Tblsp. sugar
2 tsp. salt
3 cups warm water
4 Tblsp. margarine

Mix dry milk with warm water. Add yeast to 1 cup of the warm milk and dissolve; let stand 5 minutes. Add remaining milk, salt, sugar and margarine; mix well. Stir in flour 1 cup at a time, until thoroughly blended. The dough should make a soft ball. Turn out onto a floured board and coat the dough lightly with flour. Knead 8 to 10 minutes or use dough hooks with electric mixer until dough is no longer sticky. Place dough in a greased bowl. Turn the dough to grease all sides. Cover and let rise in a warm place until dough doubles in bulk (1 to 1½ hours). Punch down with fist and push all sides into the center of the dough. Knead for 1 or 2 minutes. Divide in half and place in greased bread pans. Let rise until 1 inch above the top of the pan. Bake at 350° for 40-50 minutes. Remove from pans and brush with margarine. Cool on rack.   **Cost per loaf: 81¢**

175

Sourdough

The yeast in most home-made bread adds about half the cost. But what if you didn't need to buy yeast? What about "growing" your own? Most recipes point out that it takes a real knack to succeed with sourdough, and, as the *Joy of Cooking* puts it, "the starter must be cosseted along." But don't let that discourage you from trying. Collect sourdough information from every cookbook you can find and experiment for the best results in your climate.

Sourdough Starter

1 pkg. dry yeast (1 Tblsp.)
1 cup all-purpose flour
1 pinch sugar
1 cup luke-warm (*not hot*) water
(not tap water if it's chlorinated)

Add the flour, sugar, yeast, and water to a glass jar (1-quart or larger) and mix with a wooden or plastic spoon—never use metal with your yeast mixture. Cover the top of the jar with a sock or other clean cloth (it needs to breathe). Put a rubber band around the jar at the top of the batter, so you can see it grow as it's working.

The sourdough should begin to rise and bubble. Let it sit on your counter doing its thing at room temperature for at least six hours. You can even let it sit for a full day. Then, unless you are going to make bread right away, store your sourdough jar in the refrigerator. Your bread will have a better flavor after the starter has had a day or two to "ripen." The only hard part is to remember to take the sourdough starter out of the refrigerator about two hours before you need to use it—so it can start working again.

When you take a cupful of starter for baking, there will be some left in the jar. Add one cup of flour, a pinch of sugar, and one cup of luke-warm water back into the jar. Mix everything well and let it sit on the counter for 12 hours or more before returning the jar to the refrigerator. If, after several uses, your starter isn't rising above the rubber band, it's worn out—and your bread won't rise either. Time to start over.

Cost for one cup of starter once you've got it going: 10¢ or less

Sourdough White Bread in a Bread-Maker

I'm not only cheap, I live a busy life with kids and a job. I make bread by hand, but the ease of the bread-making machine is seducing. Home-made bread with only five minutes of preparation time, including replenishing the sourdough starter! How can anyone resist? And the saving on home-made bread would pay for the machine in less than a year. However, I am *not* telling you to rush out and buy a bread machine. I don't have one because I'm too cheap to buy one, and Santa hasn't gotten the message yet. (The following recipe was contributed by my editor, just in case the jolly old elf comes through this year.)

Make sure the sourdough starter has had two hours to reach room temperature. Then stir before measuring out the needed portion. In the bread machine bucket, add:

> 2 cups flour
> 1 Tblsp. sugar
> 1 tsp. salt
> (2-3 Tblsp. powdered milk)
> 1 Tblsp. shortening
> 1 cup sourdough starter
> ½ cup warm (*not hot*) water

Punch the button or set the timer, and your bread is in motion. Then replenish the starter before you forget, and wait at least 24 hours before using the starter again. **Cost: 33¢**

Sourdough Onion Rolls

Add one grated onion (or other favorite herbs) to the sourdough white bread mix. Let the bread-maker do the kneading and first rising, about one hour. Take the dough out and shape into rolls. Let rise again in a warm place (80°) until almost doubled in bulk—an hour or more. Bake in the oven at 350° for 30 minutes or until golden brown. **Cost: 37¢**

177

Pie Crust Mix

This recipe can be prepared easily ahead of time. It is about the right amount for five double-crust pies or ten single crusts.

10 cups sifted flour
3⅓ cups shortening
5 tsp. salt

Combine sifted flour and salt. Cut in shortening with pastry cutter, fork, or two knives until the mixture is crumbly and the pieces of shortening are smaller than split peas. Store in a sealed container in the refrigerator.   **Cost: $1.85**

Pie Crust
(using the mix)

Combine 2⅔ cups of mix with 5 to 7 Tblsp. of cold water sprinkled on top. Toss together with a fork until all the mixture is moistened. Form into 2 balls, flatten, and roll between 2 sheets of waxed paper (lightly floured) or roll out on a floured pastry sheet using a rolling pin cover. To transfer to pie pan, remove the top sheet of waxed paper, leaving the pastry sheet or bottom paper in place. Fold the pastry in half and then remove sheet from top half and use the paper or pastry sheet to fold the pastry into quarters. Remove the pastry sheet. Place the point of the wedge of pie pastry at the center of the pie pan and unfold. Lift gently at the ends to fit the pastry to the sides and bottom of the pan. This recipe makes two single crusts or one double-crust pie. To bake unfilled, prick dough with fork tines, and bake at 450° for approximately 10 minutes. **Cost: 37¢**

Note: Experienced cooks will find the above recipe to be easy, fast, and cheap. But if you're new to cooking, and intimidated by pie crusts, check out the next page. Costs a little more, but absolutely fool-proof!

Fool-proof Pie Crust

4 cups flour
2 tsp. salt
1¾ cups shortening
1 egg
1 Tblsp. vinegar
4 Tblsp. cold water

Mix flour, salt, and shortening with a fork until crumbly and well-blended. Mix egg, vinegar, and water in a small cup or bowl, then add to flour. Add more water if needed to hold clumps together. This should handle like play-dough and it's almost impossible to ruin it—even when using up the trimmings for rerolling cinnamon swirls! Makes two pies.   **Cost per pie: 45¢**

Cinnamon Swirls

leftover pie crust trimmings
margarine
cinnamon
sugar

Using pie crust scraps, roll out leftover dough in a rectangle. Spread lightly with margarine and dust with cinnamon sugar. Roll up, jelly-roll style, and cut in ¼-inch slices. Lay on greased cookie sheet and bake for 10 minutes or so, just until golden brown, while your pie is baking.

Bread Crumb Crust

10 or so stale bread ends, toasted lightly
½ stick of margarine, melted
1 tsp. garlic powder, *or*
2 Tblsp. sugar (for desserts)

Crumb the toast in a food processor. Add melted margarine, flavoring, and mix well. Press into an 8-inch or 9-inch pie plate and chill before using for a cold filling. For a warm filling, bake crust for 10 minutes in 350° oven before using. (If you were going to throw away the bread crusts, this recipe is almost free. I hoard mine in a bag in the freezer.)   **Cost: 4¢**

Sauces and Gravy

(Also see white sauce recipes on pages 135-136.)

Cheap Chip Dip

½ cup milk
1½ Tblsp. vinegar
1 cup mayonnaise
1½ tsp. tarragon
1 tsp. dill seeds, crushed
½ tsp. garlic powder
salt & pepper to taste
1 tsp. unflavored gelatin
(*or* lemon-flavored gelatin)
1 Tblsp. hot water

Mix vinegar with milk and allow to stand for 5 minutes. Blend milk into mayonnaise. Add spices and blend. Dissolve gelatin in hot water and add to mayonnaise mixture. Chill for 1-2 hours. Makes approximately 1¾ cups. Use for dip with potato chips or fresh vegetables. **Cost: 59¢**

Variation: Omit garlic powder and tarragon and add 2 finely chopped green onions or ¼ cup minced chives.

Garlic Mayo

This will put "zing" into your snacks!

half of a quart jar of mayonnaise
4-5 large cloves of garlic, crushed

This is ideal if you have a half-used jar of mayonnaise. Mix the pressed garlic into the mayonnaise. Refrigerate for at least a day before using, to get the full flavor. Use as a veggie dip, on baked fish or chicken, or on sandwiches. It tastes like a high-priced gourmet treat. **Cost: 70¢**

Curried Mayo

½ cup of mayonnaise
1 heaping tsp. curry

Mix and use in egg salad sandwiches, as a veggie dip, or on baked chicken and fish. **Cost: 67¢**

Homemade Mayonnaise

2 eggs
2 Tblsp. vinegar
2 Tblsp. vegetable oil
1 tsp. salt
2 Tblsp. prepared mustard
2½ cups vegetable oil

Prepare in food processor, blender, or with electric mixer. Combine eggs, vinegar, 2 Tblsp. oil, salt, and mustard. Blend on high for 1 minute. Without stopping the mixer, *slowly trickle* the 2½ cups of vegetable oil into the container. Do not stop blending until all of the oil is absorbed and the mayonnaise is set and slightly firm. Yields about 1 quart. **Cost: $1.31**

Cost of 1 qt. house-brand mayo: $1.49

"Cooked" Mayonnaise

1½ cups water
5 Tblsp. flour
2 egg yolks
2 Tblsp. sugar
2 Tblsp. dry mustard
1 tsp. salt
¾ cup oil
¼ cup vinegar

In blender or food processor, beat well the last six ingredients. Then mix the flour and water in a saucepan and cook until thick and almost translucent, stirring constantly. A whisk works well. Slowly pour hot flour-and-water sauce into egg mixture while beating on high speed. Makes 3 cups of silky smooth mayo. **Cost: 56¢**

Herb Vinegars

Save some of your one-pint or one-quart bottles, preferably those with small necks. Soak off labels and add your own for each kind of vinegar you plan to "brew." Basil, rosemary, tarragon, thyme, and dill are excellent herbs to use, but get fresh or dried herbs, if you can, rather than powdered. For garlic vinegar, use three or more fresh garlic cloves, mashed. Or try mint vinegar, to use in coleslaw. Ginger vinegar (mince the root) lends a nice zing to a fruit salad dressing. If you are artistic, a classy-looking label will make your gourmet vinegars an inexpensive but clever gift, for about 40¢ a pint.

Put an ounce or so of the herb into each bottle. The more you use, the stronger the flavor—there's no magic formula. Fill with *cider* vinegar and let sit for a week before using. If you are planning several of these, buy your vinegar by the gallon for the lowest prices.

Salad Dressing

If you use a low-cost vegetable oil for salad dressing (rather than olive oil), the herb vinegars hide your choice pretty well.

⅓ cup vinegar
⅔ cup vegetable oil
pinch sugar
salt and pepper
(paprika)

Mix well and refrigerate.   Cost: 42¢

183

Salads

Potato Salad

6 large boiled potatoes, cubed
6 hard boiled eggs, chopped
1 large onion, chopped
1 dill pickle, chopped
  or 2 Tblsp. relish
1½ cups mayonnaise
2 Tblsp. prepared mustard
2 Tblsp. vinegar *or* pickle brine

Combine potatoes, eggs, onion, and pickle. Mix mayonnaise, mustard and vinegar or brine. Add to potato mixture. Mix well and chill. Makes about 8 cups. (With some additional veggies such as carrot sticks, this can make a full meal.)   **Cost: $1.27**

Bean Salad

1 can green beans (15 oz.)
1 can yellow wax beans (15 oz.)
1 can kidney beans, drained (15 oz.)
1 large onion, sliced
1 cup vegetable oil
⅓ cup vinegar
1 tsp. oregano
1 tsp. garlic powder
1 tsp. crushed dill seed
salt & pepper to taste

Combine the green beans, yellow wax beans, kidney beans, and onions (sliced approximately ¼-inch thick and separated into rings) in a large covered bowl. Combine the vinegar, oil, and spices. Add to bean mixture. Marinate overnight in refrigerator.   **Cost: $2.14**

Macaroni Salad

2 cups macaroni
6-8 cups water
1 Tblsp. salt
6 hard-boiled eggs, chopped
1 medium dill pickle, chopped
    or 2 Tblsp. relish
1 onion, chopped
¼ cup green or red pepper, chopped
1½ cups mayonnaise
2 Tblsp. prepared mustard
2 tsp. vinegar or dill pickle brine

Cook the macaroni in boiling water with 1 Tblsp. salt until tender. Drain well and chill. Add chopped egg, pickle, onion, and sweet peppers. Toss to mix. Combine mayonnaise, mustard, and vinegar or pickle brine. Add to macaroni-vegetable mixture. Mix well and chill. Makes about 6 cups.   **Cost: $1.51**

Coleslaw

½ medium head cabbage
1 large carrot
1 medium onion
1½ cups mayonnaise
3-4 Tblsp. sugar
3-4 Tblsp. vinegar
½ tsp. salt

Finely shred the cabbage, carrot, and onion. Mix well. Combine mayonnaise, sugar, vinegar, and salt. Add to shredded vegetables and chill.   **Cost: $1.01**

Tomato Salad with Basil

4 large peeled tomatoes
salt & pepper to taste
1 Tblsp. wine vinegar
2 Tblsp. oil
⅓ cup fresh basil leaves

Dice tomatoes and combine with salt, pepper, vinegar and oil. Stack the basil leaves and cut them lengthwise in thin strips. Mix with tomato mixture and serve.

Cost from the store rather than garden: $1.45

Variation: Add cubes of mozzarella cheese.

Desserts

One way to cut your kitchen time as well as your budget is to skip desserts except for special occasions. Leaving the table with sugar-coated teeth isn't a great idea—we probably should eat dessert first, and finish up with celery sticks! Wouldn't the kids like that?

Baked Apples

4-6 apples
brown sugar
cinnamon
dab of margarine
½ cup water

This is the perfect dessert to make—if you're having one—when you already plan to use the oven. Wash and core the apples. Spoon a bit of brown sugar into the center hole and sprinkle with cinnamon. Dab a tiny bit of margarine on top. Place in a brownie pan or other oven-proof dish and add the water. Bake at 350° or so for 45 minutes. **Cost: 78¢**

Crystallized Grapes and Oranges

3 cups seedless grapes
(try using several varieties)
2 oranges or tangerines cut in wedges or slices
1 egg white
1 cup granulated sugar

Lightly beat the egg white. Roll fruit pieces in egg white, then roll in sugar. Let dry and serve. This is a particularly attractive dessert for holidays. **Cost: $1.47**

Whenever you have egg yolks left from one recipe, cover the yolks with milk or water in a cup and save to use in a quiche or other egg-based meal. Easily frozen, as well.

187

Fruit Cobbler

3-4 cups* of ripe fruit (diced)
½ cup any fruit juice
1 Tblsp. cornstarch
    (*or* 1 Tblsp. tapioca, *or* 2 Tblsp. flour)
sugar
cinnamon, ginger, nutmeg, or grated
    lemon/orange rind
1 biscuit recipe (page 172)

Spread fruit in bottom of baking dish. Dissolve cornstarch in juice and pour over fruit. Add extra sugar only if the fruit is not very sweet by itself. Sprinkle with spices. Place dish in heated oven (350°) while mixing the biscuits (or at least 20 minutes). Add 2 Tblsp. of sugar to the biscuit mix and drop by spoonfuls over the now-hot fruit. Return to the oven at 350° for 10 minutes or until golden brown.   **Cost: $1.06**

*If you do not have quite enough fruit, extend the amount with diced stale bread but be sure to include spices and a bit of extra sugar.

Quick Whip Pudding

1 small (3 oz.) package any flavor gelatin
½ cup boiling water
1 cup well-drained crushed ice

Chill 4 half-cup dessert dishes in the freezer. Place gelatin in blender. Add boiling water. Blend 2 minutes. With blender still running, add well-drained crushed ice. Continue to blend until container feels cool. Pour into chilled dishes and refrigerate until serving.   **Cost: 37¢**

Scottish Shortbread

1 cup margarine (or butter)
½ cup sugar
2½ cups sifted flour

Cream the margarine with sugar. Add flour. Chill. Pat into two 7-inch circles and mark 16 wedges in each. Bake at 300° for 30 minutes.   **Cost: 49¢**

Pudding Mix

3⅓ cups dry milk
2½ tsp. salt
1 Tblsp. corn starch
1⅔ cups sugar

Combine dry ingredients and store in a tightly closed container. Makes enough for 4 batches of pudding (see below). **Cost: $1.04**

For **Vanilla Pudding,** combine 1¼ cups mix with 1¾ cups water. Cook over low heat to a boil, stirring constantly. Boil gently for 2 minutes. Add 1 tsp. vanilla. Chill until set. For **Chocolate Pudding,** add 4 Tblsp. cocoa to dry ingredients before mixing.
Cost for Vanilla: 21¢. For Chocolate: 46¢

Old-fashioned Rice Pudding

½ cup raw rice
4 cups milk
½ tsp. cinnamon, nutmeg
¼ cup sugar (white or brown)
½ tsp. salt
(½ cup raisins)

Combine all ingredients and pour into a greased baking dish. Bake for 3 hours in a slow oven (about 300°), stirring several times during the first hour. The mixture should not boil. Serve either hot or cold. **Cost: 69¢**

Brownie Mix

5 cups sugar
3¾ cups sifted flour
2 cups cocoa

Combine the above ingredients and store in a covered container.
Cost: $2.88

For **Brownies,** Melt 1 stick (½ cup) of margarine. Add 1 cup plus 1 Tblsp. of brownie mix and 2 eggs, beating well after each egg. Add 1 cup plus 1 Tblsp. more of mix, plus 1 tsp. vanilla. If desired, add ½ cup chopped walnuts. Spread in a well-greased 8 x 8-inch pan. Bake at 350° for 30 minutes. **Cost: 89¢**

Wacky Cake Mix

This is a quick, easy cake that has no eggs, milk, or butter, so it may be a good choice for those with allergies or who are on cholesterol-guarded diets. The mix is enough for 3 cakes.

7¼ cups flour
1 cup cocoa
2½ tsp. salt
5 tsp. baking soda
5 cups sugar

Combine all ingredients and store in a covered container.

Cost: $2.21

For **Wacky Cake**, add 2¾ cups cake mix to 1 cup cold water, 5 Tblsp. vegetable oil, 1 tsp. vanilla, and 1 Tblsp. vinegar. Bake in an 8 x 8-inch lightly greased pan at 350° for 30 minutes.   Cost: 74¢

Sponge Cake

1⅛ cups flour
½ tsp. salt
¾ cup sugar
¼ cup vegetable oil
6 Tblsp. cold water
2 egg yolks
4 egg whites
¾ tsp. vanilla
¼ tsp. almond extract
1½ tsp. baking powder
¼ tsp. cream of tartar

Sift flour, salt, baking powder, and sugar. Make a well and add oil, water, yolks, and flavoring. Beat egg whites with cream of tartar until stiff. Fold into cake mixture; pour into 9-inch greased spring-form pan or Bundt pan. Bake at 325° until top springs back, about 45 minutes.   Cost: 66¢

Miscellaneous

Red Beet Jelly

1½ lbs. beets
½ cup lemon juice
2 boxes dried pectin
1 3-oz. package flavored red gelatin
8 cups sugar
water

To loosen the skins, boil the beets for approximately 5 minutes, leaving tap roots and an inch or two of the tops in place. Remove from the boiling water and peel, removing the tops. Discard water. Slice beets, and cover with fresh water. Cook until tender. Use 6 cups of the beet juice (add more water if necessary to make 6 cups). Add lemon juice, pectin, and the flavored gelatin. Bring to a boil, add sugar, and return to a rolling boil. Remove from heat and let stand for 3 to 5 minutes. Skim off the top. Pour into hot scalded jars. Cover with paraffin or seal with lids.   **Cost: $5.27**

Dandelion Wine

1 qt. yellow dandelion blossoms
1 gal. boiling water
1 pkg. yeast
4 lbs. sugar
1 orange (sliced)
1 slice lemon

Wash blossoms thoroughly. Put in boiling water and let stand 4 minutes. Remove and discard blossoms. Let water cool to lukewarm. Add yeast, sugar, orange and lemon slices. Let stand and stir every day until it stops "working" (bubbling), about 10 days to 2 weeks. Siphon off and run through cheese cloth (bottom will be thick). Bottle and let rest for at least a week for best flavor.
Cost per gallon: $1.55

191

Beet Wine

2 doz. medium sized beets
22 cups water
6 cups sugar (+ ½ cup for a sweeter wine)
1 box raisins (15 oz.)
3 pkgs. yeast

Cut beets in half or quarters. Bring to a boil, and simmer for one hour. In a crock (larger than 1 gal.), put the sugar and raisins. Pour hot beet juice into the crock, and stir to dissolve the sugar. When it has cooled to lukewarm, stir in the 3 packages of yeast. Stir once a day for 13-14 days. (If you let it stand too long, it will turn to vinegar.) Siphon or filter into quart bottles. Fill right up into the necks. Cap and let rest for a month for best flavor. Makes about 4 quarts. (Use beets in a salad or as a vegetable. Raisins can be used to make a potent and tangy chutney, but rinse off yeast first.) **Cost per gallon: $2.88 not counting temporary use of beets.**

Homemade Yogurt

1 qt. milk
3 Tblsp. plain yogurt
(store-bought or from last batch)

Bring milk to boil over moderate heat stirring constantly. Cool milk to 95°-110°. Remove skin. Whisk yogurt into milk and mix well. Divide into 4 1-cup jars. Cover tightly and incubate at 100° until proper consistency, 4 to 5 hours. (To get a 100° environment, place yogurt brew in oven with pilot light or place on a heating pad at medium heat.) **Cost: 63¢**

Finger Gelatin

1 can (12 oz.) any frozen juice, thawed
3 envelopes gelatin
1 can hot water

Soften gelatin in juice. Add hot water and stir until gelatin is dissolved. Pour into a greased 9 x 13-inch pan. Chill until well set. Cut into squares or shapes—a high-protein snack. **Cost: $1.94**

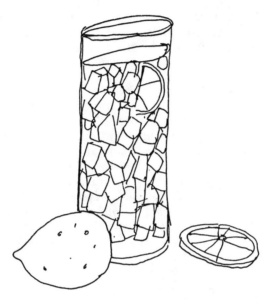

Beverages

In a society that seems addicted to expensive soft drinks, a trip to the grocery store can wreck the food budget, starting in the cola aisle. Because those purchases would be empty calories—a nutritional disaster—here are some other low-cost alternatives to juice and milk, some of which might even be good for you. (By keeping a jug-full in the refrigerator, you can waylay the urge to buy more expensive drinks.)

One gadget that can be useful (if you can afford it) is a juicer. You can make your own fruit and vegetable juices almost instantly, and they're a delicious, healthful alternative to commercial drinks. Most people like blender drinks, too.

193

Mint Iced Tea

Mint grows wild in many parts of the country and can be found in moist meadow areas. The mint family is distinguished by its square stem and its strong flavor. It is incredibly easy to grow—there are many varieties—and a sprig of mint in a sick-room or gift bouquet gives a special touch. If you don't already have a mint patch in your yard, try to plan one next year—barter with a friend or scavenge the wilds. (Buy, if you have to.) Even when you buy dried mint leaves at a co-op, it's not too expensive. Store dried mint in a closed jar or bagged in the freezer.

For iced tea, use a generous handful of leaves for each pitcher of tea. Pour boiling water to half-way and steep for 30 minutes. If you have a sweet tooth, add honey to the water while it's still hot. Fill remainder of pitcher with cold water or ice cubes and refrigerate. (*Caution: pregnant women should avoid mint. There is a small chance that it could contribute to a miscarriage.* On the other hand, a mint drink may start the menstrual flow for a woman who is irregular.) **Cost per quart with honey: 25¢**

Shrubs

A "shrub"—a cooling drink made with fruit, vinegar, and honey—is considered by many to be an herbal and nutritional remedy for a variety of ailments, according to Mary Carse's book, *Herbs of the Earth* (Upper Access, 1989). If nothing else, it's at least refreshing.

Fill a glass or ceramic container with any edible ripe berries you have, even choke cherries or elderberries. Add enough cider vinegar to cover. Let stand for ten days to two weeks. (A towel over the top will keep the flies away.) Discard the fruit or use for chutney. Measure the remaining liquid and add an equal amount of honey before bottling. (No need to process—the vinegar and honey take care of that.) Use the syrup—about a ¼-cupful—for each glass of ice water or mug of hot water.

Cost per quart if berries are free: 50¢

Quencher

1 Tblsp. *cider* vinegar
1 Tblsp. honey
1 glass of cold water

Sort of a shrub quickie. Dr. Jarvis recommends this in his book *Folk Medicine* (Fawcett Crest, 1961) for everything from high blood pressure to arthritis. For someone trying to skip alcoholic beverages, the tang in this drink will be quite appealing.

Cost per quart: about 24¢

Shandy-gaff

Invigorating and good for the digestion, they say.

2 tsp. ground ginger
  (*or* 3 inches of ginger root, minced)
2 Tblsp. grated lemon rind
  (about 1 lemon's worth)
4 Tblsp. honey
2 qts. boiling water

Mix and steep. Can be served hot, or chilled for an iced drink.

Cost per quart: about 15¢, not counting lemon rind

Orange Spice Tea

Use your leftover orange and lemon rinds. Mince finely and dry or freeze. Use 1 scant teaspoonful in a tea strainer with 1 clove (or dash of ground cloves). Steep in hot water and serve. Can be chilled for an iced drink, too.

Cost per quart: 5¢ for cloves

Instant Breakfast Drink

1 banana, peeled
1 egg
¼ cup dry milk
1 cup cold water
capful vanilla or almond extract
1-2 ice cubes

Mix in blender.

Cost per serving: 20¢

Resources

Newsletters

The Banker's Secret Bulletin (quarterly), Good Advice Press, Box 78, Elizaville, NY 12523. 1-800-255-0899. $19.95 per year. This newsletter is geared to helping you save money on just about anything—from mortgage payments to fuel oil to probate. A little pricey for 32 pages a year, but each eight-page issue is packed with timely information that ought to save you more than as you spend. Sample copy $1. (Share a subscription with a friend and cut the price in half.)

Living Cheap News (ten times a year), Box 700058, San Jose, CA 95170. $12 year. Sample copy $1 plus business-size SASE. A friendly discussion with the reader on money saving attitudes and ideas. Not as crammed with specific tips as some of the other newsletters but provocative reading, anyway.

The Penny Pincher (bimonthly), P.O. Box 809, Kings Park, NY 11754. $12 per year. Sample copy for a 29¢ stamp and your address. Includes a column on "Cheap Food! Good Food!" Lots of other helpful columns and articles, too, with a myriad of resource contacts and addresses in this 12-page newsletter.

The Tightwad Gazette (monthly), RR 1, Box 3570, Leeds, ME 04263-9710. $12 per year. A thoughtful and well-researched compendium of money-saving ideas: on food, gift-giving, and just about anything around the house. You could send $1 for a sample, but why bother? Go ahead and subscribe to this 8-page monthly. You could save much more than that in the first few months.

Books

Cheap Tricks by Andy Dappen. 1992, Brier Books, Mountlake Terrace, Washington 98043. 405 pages, paperback. $13.95 plus shipping. Call 1-800-356-9315. Witty, irreverent, and full of useful bits of "cheap" information on just about everything: from babies to funerals—and including food.

More-With-Less Cookbook by Doris Janzen Longacre. 1976, Herald Press, Scottdale, PA 15683. 328 pages, comb-bound paperback. $14.95 plus $2 shipping. Order from the Profident Bookstore, 1625 Lititz Pike, Lancaster, PA 17601-6599 or call 1-800-759-4447. The subtitle says it all: "Suggestions by Mennonites on how to eat better and consume less of the world's limited food resources." Excellent! (More than 500,000 have been printed since 1976.)

Recipe Index

Recipe Index

About the Author

Pat Edwards lives in Ohio with her husband and two sons. After graduation from high school, Pat worked for two years as a free-lance reporter for a local newspaper. A licensed social worker with more than 16 years experience, Pat has demonstrated a life-long interest in Home Economics. Three years of experience as a house mother for troubled kids has provided her with a wealth of experience in working with the conflicts between budgets and personalities. More than 20 years of marriage has provided her with a proving ground for living on a budget while remaining happily healthy.

In her first book, *Cheap Eating,* Pat has combined her love of writing with her zest for "beating the system" in a fun and easy-reading guide.

Upper Access selects nonfiction books to improve the quality of life. Please call or write for our catalog.

Upper Access Books
One Upper Access Road
P.C. Box 457
Hinesburg, Vermont 05461
802-482-2988
1-800-356-9315